School Testing

SCHOOL TESTING

What Parents and Educators Need to Know

Estelle S. Gellman

PRAEGER

Westport, Connecticut
London

Library of Congress Cataloging-in-Publication Data

Gellman, Estelle S.
    School testing : what parents and educators need to know / Estelle
S. Gellman.
      p.   cm.
    Includes bibliographical references (p.   ) and index.
    ISBN 0–275–94800–5 (alk. paper)
    1. Educational tests and measurements. 2. Examinations—Validity.
3. Examinations—Interpretation.   I. Title
LB3051.G365   1995
371.2′6—dc20   94–28003

British Library Cataloguing in Publication Data is available.

Library of Congress Catalog Card Number: 94–28003
ISBN: 0–275–94800–5

First published in 1995

Praeger Publishers, 88 Post Road West, Westport, CT 06881
An imprint of Greenwood Publishing Group, Inc.

Printed in the United States of America

The paper used in this book complies with the
Permanent Paper Standard issued by the National
Information Standards Organization (Z39.48–1984).

10 9 8 7 6 5 4 3 2

To Doug, Russell, and Beth, whose experiences
were the impetus for this undertaking, and to
Yale, without whose support it could not have
been realized.

Contents

Illustrations

FIGURES

TABLES

Preface

In recent years we have seen an increased emphasis on school testing. Our schools are being held accountable for ensuring that students are in fact learning what they should be learning, and test results are used to demonstrate their success.

Standardized test scores are routinely reported in the media, and the comparative success of different groups of students is widely publicized. Unfortunately, however, these reports are rarely accompanied by an explanation of what the tests are actually testing or what the test scores mean. The scores of individual students are also reported to educators and parents as a way of informing them of student progress. Again, however, these reports provide minimal explanation of the meaning of the scores.

It is the purpose of this book to provide the information that parents and educators need in order to interpret and evaluate test results. I have attempted to present this information in a manner that can be easily understood without a background in educational measurement and statistics. At the same time, however, I have also tried to provide comprehensive coverage of the basic concepts underlying educational measurement and statistics.

I don't want simply to say what I think ought to be, but to enable both parents and educators to evaluate the information for themselves. Toward this end, Chapters 2 and 3 may include more than anyone ever thought they wanted to know about reliability and validity. I strongly believe, however, that these concepts must be understood before we can fully appreciate what test scores tell us. I urge the reader not to skip these chapters, but to try to grasp these concepts. If Chapter 3 becomes too cumbersome, the material on the different types of reliability coefficients may be omitted; the concept of measurement error, however, is crucial to score interpretation.

Chapters 4, 5, 6, and 7 describe the different types of tests typically administered in the schools. In a book of this size it is impossible to describe all of the tests that might be given. Instead, I have tried to distinguish among the different categories of tests and to provide examples typical of each. This chapter should provide the information needed to identify the major types of tests given to your children and to understand the type of information they provide.

Chapters 8 and 9 focus on score interpretation. Grade scores, percentile ranks, stanines, and NCE scores are among the many kinds of test scores that are reported. It is necessary to differentiate among these different types of scores in order to understand the information each provides. As discussed in Chapter 10, however, it is not enough simply to understand the meaning of the score; when we use test scores as the basis for educational decisions, we must also evaluate the test and see that the results are used appropriately.

I bring to this project not only my experience as a professor of educational measurement for close to three decades, but also my experiences as a parent of three children. It is the latter that has convinced me of the need for this book. I have too often seen both parents and educators place too much importance on a single test score. If this book provides the information needed to put tests and test scores in proper perspective, it will fulfill an important function. Test scores are here to stay; it is up to both parents and educators to see that they are used responsibly. I hope that this book will provide a measure of support in that endeavor.

To the extent that this goal is met, I owe a debt of gratitude to my friends and colleagues who gave so generously of their time to read and comment on my early efforts. In particular, I would like to thank Mina Berkowitz, Ruth Davis, Yale H. Gellman, Ruth F. Gold, Gerald H. Grayson, William J. McKeough, William Shine, and Ralph Zalma. They helped me to see what others didn't see, kept me from straying too far afield, and showed me how best to say what I had to say.

School Testing

Chapter 1

What Can We Learn from Testing?

Do you remember what it's like to take a test? Do you remember waiting nervously for the test to begin, worried about what it would cover and whether or not you would remember all you had studied? If you're like most of us, you can probably remember at least one test where you really thought you knew the work but the test wasn't on what was covered in class, was so confusing that you couldn't figure out what you were supposed to do, or focused on the one little area that you hadn't reviewed. Perhaps you can remember another time when the test seemed fine, but you didn't do your best because you couldn't concentrate on your work. You had a splitting headache, or a stomachache, or you were too excited about being in the play or going to camp or going out on a special date. Can you also remember a time when you knew you received a higher score than you deserved and your classmates, who really knew the work better, got lower grades? Most people who have gone through school have had these types of experiences; they occur because tests are not perfect. They do not provide infallible measures of our abilities.

Why, then, are children so often tested in school? Even though tests are fallible, they can provide useful information about your child. Teachers give tests to assess how well their students have learned the material that was taught and to help them diagnose each student's strengths and weaknesses.

Classroom tests can help a teacher determine which children have mastered a particular skill. A poor score on a test may alert a teacher to a misconception or misunderstanding that was not previously apparent in class. Test scores can help teachers assess the accuracy of their impressions as well as indicate areas that need closer investigation. Furthermore, although a teacher may often have the insight to know that a student has a problem in a particular area, a test can help to pinpoint the nature of the difficulty.

School districts give standardized aptitude and achievement tests to help determine where students will be placed, to find out how their students' performance compares to that of students in other districts, and to help evaluate curricula and programs. The score on a standardized test, for example, may be a major factor in the decision to place a child in a remedial reading class or an enrichment program in science. Test performance may also be a factor in program evaluation. A rise in third-grade reading scores, for example, may indicate that a new curriculum has been effective, while relatively low scores in writing may indicate that curriculum development is needed in this area. Similarly, when the children in a particular school or school district do consistently worse on standardized tests than do the children in other comparable districts, the test performance may serve as a warning and an impetus for change.

Test performance is also a factor in selection decisions that may determine the future educational options available to a child. Tests are used, for example, in determining who will be admitted to special schools or colleges, who will be selected for awards or scholarships, and who will be selected for special programs within a school.

Most children spend at least twelve years in school, and important decisions concerning the education they receive and the programs available in their schools are often based on the results of tests. Although many of these decisions are based on a combination of factors, including classroom performance and teacher recommendations, test performance is usually given considerable weight. While teacher recommendations and school grades vary with the teacher, tests are seen as a means of evaluating all of the candidates on a single measuring scale.

It is important to remember that although tests can contribute valuable information about a student, the use of test scores in decision making must be tempered by an understanding of the limitations inherent in the scores. A test score must be considered in conjunction with all the other information that we know about a child, and major decisions should not be based on the score of a single isolated test. All too often, however, we see tests used as though they provide the irrefutable truth about a child's ability. We even occasionally see school districts use a single test score as the basis for pivotal educational decisions.

Although of course there is a need to set standards, test scores must be put into proper perspective. We must consider the role of tests in the decision-making process as well as the nature of the information that different tests provide. It is only with an appreciation of the limitations of tests that we can reap the advantage of the information that they do provide. In order to understand these limitations, it is helpful to look at tests as measuring instruments. The same way as we look at a bathroom scale as an instrument to measure our weight, we can look at a test as an instrument to measure our skills and abilities.

MEASUREMENT AND EVALUATION

If we think of a test as a scale, we can think of a test score as a reading on the scale. Just as you get on your bathroom scale in the morning to see how much you weigh, a teacher gives a test to see where your child stands on a scale of subject-matter achievement. In the same way that you evaluate the reading on your bathroom scale and then perhaps decide to go on a diet, your child's teacher evaluates your child's test performance and decides whether the subject has been adequately mastered. Based on the teacher's evaluation of the score, your child may be assigned more work in fractions, for example, or placed in a more advanced group in reading.

In any discussion of testing, an important distinction must be made between evaluation and measurement. Evaluation is the process of arriving at a value judgment—the judgment that you are overweight and should go on a diet, for example, or the judgment that your child should be accelerated in reading. Measurement, on the other hand, is the process of obtaining a measure on a scale, the process of weighing yourself or of getting a score on a test. Measures are the readings on a scale; they provide the raw data upon which evaluations are based. Test scores are measures, and the educational decisions one arrives at on the basis of those test scores are evaluations.

When one considers many of the criticisms of testing, the concerns expressed are with how tests are used in evaluation rather than with the tests themselves. It is important to know that tests are limited. They sample one slice of behavior at one point in time. They are fallible, and any evaluation based on test scores must take that fact into account.

When we weigh ourselves, we don't criticize the scale for not also giving us our height or accurately predicting whether we will lose that extra ten pounds before the summer. Yet, we criticize tests when they measure only limited skills or do not provide information on other things we would like to know. Perhaps our criticism would be better directed at claims that the tests measure more than they do, and at those who use test scores as if they were infallible. Tests provide important information for use in evaluation, but the evaluation process must take into account the limitations of the measures on which they are based. Just as you wouldn't go on a diet because of a high reading on a broken scale, educational decisions should not be made on the basis of a test that gives inconsistent results. It is therefore as important to evaluate the test as it is to understand the meaning of the scores upon which educational decisions are made.

EVALUATING THE TEST

Before the scores on a test can be evaluated, it is important to evaluate the test itself for both accuracy and appropriateness. To continue the analogy of the bathroom scale, you certainly wouldn't trust the readings of your scale if your weight were ten pounds higher after your shower than it was before, or if it dropped twenty pounds after you finished breakfast. Such a lack of consistency would make you wonder about the accuracy of your scale, and it is unlikely that you would put very much faith in those readings.

Just as we expect our bathroom scale to give us consistent measures, we should also expect to see consistency in test scores. The technical term for test consistency is reliability, and test reliability is one of the things that should be assessed before the scores on any test are interpreted. If the test is not consistent in its measurement, differences among scores will represent random fluctuation rather than real differences in the ability or trait being measured.

If Jonathan and Jessica received scores of 80 and 90, respectively, on an arithmetic test, for example, and the test were not reliable, we could not be sure that Jonathan really knew the material any better than did Jessica. If the test were unreliable, the difference between their scores could well have been due to error on the test itself. The more error that enters into the scores, the less faith we have that, if the test were given again tomorrow, Jonathan would still do better than Jessica. The more accurate or reliable the test, the more faith we have that their performance would be consistent on subsequent testings.

The different types of error that may contribute to the unreliability of a test score will be further discussed in Chapter 3. At this point, however, it is important to recognize that even the best tests are not totally free of error, and that one important feature in evaluating a test is the degree to which the test scores are consistent over time. The more reliable a test, the more consistent the scores will be and the more likely it will be that similar scores will be obtained on subsequent testings.

Since there is error present in all of our educational measures, decisions should be made on the basis of multiple assessments wherever possible. If a child scored low in vocabulary on three different occasions, you would have more reason to believe that the child had difficulty with vocabulary than if a low score was obtained on one isolated test.

Unfortunately, however, decisions are often made on the basis of a single test score. Acceptance into a special program or the granting of a scholarship, for example, may be based on the score on a single test. For the most part, the tests that are used as the basis for these decisions are among the most accurate ones available. Nevertheless, even the most accurate tests are less than perfect. Furthermore, tests that are accurate for one group of students may not be equally accurate for another group of students.

Additionally, even if the test seems to be consistent in its measures, it may not be measuring what we think it is. Tests that purport to measure problem solving, for example, may only measure memory, and tests that purport to measure application of arithmetic concepts may actually test computational facility. Tests do not always measure what they say they measure or, in technical terms, are not always valid. Not only should we expect test scores to be accurate, but we should also expect some evidence that the test is in fact measuring the particular trait that we want it to measure.

When we speak of the validity of a test, we are speaking of the degree to which a test is valid for a particular purpose; a test that is valid in one situation may not be valid in another. An arithmetic test, for example, may be a valid measure of a child's mastery of number facts, but may not be a valid predictor of how that child will perform in elementary algebra. Similarly, a test that is valid for assessing how well a child can correct grammatical errors may not be a valid measure of a child's writing ability. When considering issues of reliability and validity, then, it is also important to consider the purpose for which the test is being given and the type of test that is appropriate for that purpose.

ACHIEVEMENT, APTITUDE, AND PERSONALITY TESTS

Most tests fall into one of the following categories:

1. Achievement Tests

2. Aptitude Tests, or

3. Tests of Personality, Interest, or Sentiment

Achievement tests are designed to measure the skills or knowledge a student has attained. They simply measure what a child can do at the time of testing, and do not purport either to assess innate ability or to predict future performance.

Most classroom tests are achievement tests. When a teacher gives a spelling test, for example, the purpose of the test is to measure how well the students have learned to spell the words they studied. The score on the test tells the teacher how many words each student spelled correctly. The score does not tell the teacher who will get 100% on next week's spelling test, nor does it assess innate spelling ability. The test simply measures how many words each student could spell at the time of the test.

Aptitude tests, on the other hand, are specifically designed to predict future performance. Although the predictions are based on present test performance, a test which claims to be an aptitude test must provide data showing that performance on the test is indeed related to the future perform- ance being predicted. The *SAT I: Reasoning Test* of the *Scholastic Assess- ment Tests (SAT)* that students take as juniors or seniors in high school, for example, is an aptitude test that is designed to predict how well a student will do in college. The prediction is based on how the student performs on the test, but extensive data have been obtained that indicate a relationship between scores on the test and later performance in college. It should be noted, however, as will be discussed more fully in later chapters, that no matter how strong a relationship exists between test performance and college achievement, there is no guarantee that a student who does poorly on the test won't be an A+ student in college or, similarly, that a student with a top score on the test won't drop out of college for failing grades. Nevertheless, if test scores are shown to be related to the future performance being predicted, we can have some degree of certainty that predictions based on the test scores will, over the long run, give better predictions than chance.

Tests of personality, interest, and sentiment include the array of tests that assess the presence or absence of different personality traits, vocational interests, and feelings. Except for interest inventories, these tests are not generally part of the regular school testing programs. They are usually reserved for special situations where problems are suspected and, in most cases, will not be given unless the situation has been discussed with the parent and parental permission has been given for the testing.

The vast majority of the tests that children take in school are achievement tests, and most of these are teacher-made tests of the material taught in a particular class. In addition, most children also take a variety of standardized achievement and aptitude tests. In addition to the basic difference between achievement and aptitude tests, there is also a difference between what is tested on a teacher-made test and standardized tests. Let us therefore consider the difference between these two types of tests.

STANDARDIZED AND TEACHER-MADE TESTS

Achievement tests are often categorized according to whether they are (a) teacher-made tests, which are constructed by a teacher or group of teachers for assessing the mastery of a particular unit that was taught, or (b) standardized tests, which are constructed by testing companies or, sometimes, state education departments for use in many school districts.

Standardized tests are called "standardized" because they are administered under the same standard conditions whenever and wherever they are given. Standardized tests may be used to assess achievement in a particular area, may be used to diagnose cognitive or emotional problems, or may be used to predict future performance in a particular area. Regardless of the purpose for which the test was designed, anyone taking a particular standardized test will receive the same instructions, will have the same amount of time to complete the test, and will have the test scored in the same way.

The administration of tests under standard conditions enables comparisons of the performance of students in different schools or school districts. If a school district wants to know how its first-grade students compare to first-grade students in other districts on beginning reading skills, for example, the district would administer a standardized reading test to its students. The scores would then be compared to the scores obtained by students in other districts taking the same test. This comparison would provide information on the relative performance of the two groups of first-graders, since both groups would have taken the same test under the same conditions.

Since standardized achievement tests are designed to be used by many school districts, they are designed to measure the broad objectives that one would expect all students to master. In most classrooms, however, the curriculum includes more than the basic skills and information included on these tests. While standardized tests are good for assessing how well the students in a particular school have attained the basic skills that one would expect all students to have learned, these tests are not appropriate measures of whether students have learned the particular skills and information that should have been learned in a particular class. While many of the standardized tests will assess map-reading skills, for example, a standardized test would not measure a child's knowledge of local geography or history. For these purposes, a teacher-made test is needed.

Teacher-made tests are tests constructed by teachers to assess the extent to which their students have learned what was taught in class. Because of the vast amount of work that must go into the validation of an aptitude test, most teacher-made tests are restricted to achievement tests. In contrast to standardized achievement tests, teacher-made tests are specifically designed to test the material taught in a particular class. Teacher-made tests may be pencil-and-paper tests or may be performance tests. Students may be asked to write an essay on a social studies topic, they may be asked to answer multiple-choice questions based on a science unit, or they may be given a performance test in laboratory skills, in gym, or in home economics. In each case, the test is prepared by the teacher and scored by the teacher. These tests are used for diagnosing students' strengths and weaknesses and often for the assignment of grades.

Because of the differences between teacher-made and standardized achievement tests, they are used for different purposes. Teacher-made tests are preferred for classroom diagnosis and the assignment of grades, while standardized tests are preferred for assessing the basic educational objectives that all students are expected to attain. There is no one type of test that is superior for all purposes. In selecting a test, the particular purpose of testing must be considered. If the purpose is to assess present attainment, an achievement test must be used. The decision as to which type of achievement test is appropriate depends on the learning to be measured. Similarly, if the purpose of testing is to predict future performance, an aptitude test must be used. Tests should not be given without a purpose, and it is the purpose of the testing that should determine the type of test to be given.

The aim of all testing is to provide measures that may be used in evaluating student performance, whether it be the performance of an individual student or a group of students. In order to arrive at an appropriate evaluation, of course, one must understand the meaning of the score. What does it mean to have a percentile rank of 80, or a standard T-score of 70? In order to evaluate the score, however, one must also be able to evaluate the test. Was the test appropriate for the purpose of testing? And was the test a good example of the type of test that was used? Did the test yield accurate scores? And did it measure what it was supposed to measure?

These are the questions that parents and educators should be able to address if they are to fully understand what test scores indicate about a child's performance. These issues will be addressed in subsequent chapters. Chapters 2 and 3 will focus on issues of reliability and validity in the evaluation of tests; Chapters 4 through 7 will more closely examine the different types of tests that are given in our schools; Chapters 8 and 9 will address the interpretation of test scores; and Chapter 10 will look at the use of test scores in making educational decisions.

In the final analysis, in order to understand the meaning of a test score, we must not only understand the meaning of the score itself but also examine why the test was given, what kind of test it was, and whether it provided a reliable and valid measure of what we wanted to know.

Chapter 2

Assessing Test Validity: Does It Measure What We Think It Does?

Imagine a child who wants to be on the school tennis team. She goes to tryouts expecting to play against the other aspirants but, much to her surprise, discovers that no one wants to see how she performs on the tennis court. Instead, various measures of stamina, of muscle strength, of flexibility and of physical conditioning are taken. Furthermore, as the result of these tests, even though she has consistently performed better than many of the students who do make the team, she is not selected. Were this scenario to occur, it would seem understandably unfair.

But why is it unfair? Would it seem fairer if the child had been rejected on the basis of her performance in a series of practice matches?

If you think about this scenario a bit, you will probably see that the issue revolves around whether the measures used in making the decision were really indicative of the child's ability as a tennis player. In technical terms, you are questioning the validity of the measures. You know that a child's ability as a tennis player is being tested when she competes in a tennis match, but you're not so sure that the other measures being used are really assessing that same ability. You might question the procedure and want to know what evidence there is that these measures do in fact measure a child's ability to play tennis.

You might similarly question the validity of the tests that children take in class. Is the reading readiness test given in kindergarten really predictive of a child's ability to profit from reading instruction? Does the weekly social studies quiz truly assess a child's understanding of the cultures being studied? These are the types of questions that are examined when we consider the validity of a test.

In certain types of assessment, we aren't too concerned about whether the instruments we use are actually measuring what they should be measuring. There would be little question about whether you were measuring what you meant to measure if, for example, in measuring speed of performance, you used a stop watch to measure how long it took for a youngster to swim five laps, or how long it took to run a mile. Similarly, you wouldn't question whether or not it was appropriate to use a measuring stick to determine a student's height or a tape measure to measure a student's waist. These instances deal with direct measurement. We can see what it is that we are measuring, and it doesn't take an expert to determine whether someone is appropriately measuring speed or size.

With many educational traits, however, it isn't so easy to figure out how to measure what we want to measure. We are dealing with indirect measurement, and questions often arise as to whether we are really measuring the trait that we think we are. Consider, for example, a test of intelligence or of reading comprehension. We can't see these traits directly and, in order to measure them, we have to determine what it is that youngsters ought to be able to do if they are intelligent or can comprehend what they read. It is when we are assessing traits such as these that questions arise regarding the appropriateness of our measures.

Yet, when parents or teachers are given scores on tests of academic traits, and when children are placed in classes or programs on the basis of tests of academic abilities, the question rarely arises as to whether the test is a good measure of the ability being assessed. We tend to assume that arithmetic tests are really measuring arithmetic ability, that reading tests are really measuring reading comprehension, and that intelligence tests are really measuring intelligence. And we assume that these tests are accurate measures of these traits. Many of the tests that are used to measure these traits are excellent instruments, but some are not. Furthermore, as stated earlier, even those that are quite good do not provide infallible measures of a child's abilities. In order to fully understand what the test scores are telling us, we must evaluate the test as well as the scores.

When evaluating a test, we look for evidence of two qualities: validity and reliability. The validity of a test refers to whether or not the test is measuring what it says it is, while the reliability of a test refers to how accurately the test is measuring whatever it is that it is measuring. A good test possesses both qualities; neither quality alone is sufficient. If either of these qualities is lacking, the score may be meaningless. Let's first consider the question of validity.

The question of whether or not a test is testing what it should be testing is evaluated in relationship to the purpose for which the test is being given. A test that is valid in one situation may not be valid when used for a different purpose or for testing different youngsters. Before we can assess the validity of a test, then, we have to know the purpose for which the test is being given.

If the purpose of testing is to assess your child's current knowledge or skill in a particular content area, then an achievement test should be used. If the purpose of testing is to predict how your child will perform in the future, an aptitude test is needed. Alternatively, if the purpose of testing is to assess your child's interests or describe your child's personality or feelings, then a test of personality, interests, or sentiment should be used. Not only are different types of tests appropriate for different purposes, but each type of test requires different evidence of validity. Achievement tests must have content validity, aptitude tests must have predictive validity, and tests of traits and interests must have construct validity.

ACHIEVEMENT TESTS: CONTENT VALIDITY

In order to evaluate the validity of an achievement test, we must know whether the test items adequately represent the content area that is being assessed. This type of validity is referred to as content validity, or face validity.

Consider, for example, an arithmetic test that is designed to assess a child's ability to add and subtract double digit numbers and to apply this skill to the solution of word problems. In assessing the validity of this test, several things would be evaluated. First, all of the items would be checked to make sure that they involved addition or subtraction of double digit numbers. Items that required multiplication or division, or the addition of triple digit numbers, would detract from the validity of the test. It would not be enough, however, merely to be sure that all of the items involved addition or subtraction of double digit numbers. You would also want to be sure that a variety of double digit numbers was included on the test. After all, it wouldn't really be a comprehensive test of the ability to add and subtract double digit numbers if the test was composed of only the following four items:

Add:	11	12	Subtract:	11	12
	+<u>11</u>	+<u>11</u>		−<u>11</u>	−<u>11</u>

You would not only want to see some problems using other numbers, but you would also want to make sure that the test included problems that involved "carrying" and "borrowing," that the test included an adequate number of both addition and subtraction problems, and that there were indeed word problems requiring the application of these skills. In other words, you would want to be certain that the domain of all possible numbers was adequately represented on the test and that items were included that measured all of the skills to be tested. The test would have content validity to the extent that these criteria were met.

The degree of content validity is not expressed as a number. Instead, content validity is a subjective assessment based on a comparison between the items on the test and the content areas that the test purports to measure. The standardized achievement tests published by large testing companies are usually accompanied by manuals that break down the items according to the content area and the skills being assessed. A review of the information in the test manual can give you an idea of what the test covers, although an inspection of the test items themselves is necessary in order to assess whether the items really do measure what they are said to measure. On a teacher-made test, content validity is assessed by comparing the content of the test items with an analysis of the content and skills covered in the unit being tested.

As mentioned above, however, a test cannot have content validity in the abstract. A test can be judged to be a valid test of basic arithmetic computation skills and still not be a valid test of the unit on addition and subtraction of double digit numbers that your child just covered in class. If your child's class did not cover subtraction with a zero, or addition with "carrying," or subtraction with "borrowing," then a test that covers this material is not a valid measure of the specific knowledge and abilities learned in that unit.

Similarly, a standardized test of science achievement will not be a valid measure of what your child has learned in school if the content of the test does not parallel what was taught. That very same test may be quite valid for the eighth-graders in a neighboring school, however, where different material was emphasized. Alternatively, that same test may be judged as a valid test of the basic skills that all eighth-graders should have covered in the state curriculum. The judgment of the validity of the test will vary with the purpose for which the test is used.

Consider, for example, the standardized achievement tests that most children take in school. These tests may be designed by the city or state or, perhaps, selected by your school district from those designed by different test publishers to assess performance in various subjects. These tests will usually have content validity for assessing basic skills in various curriculum areas but will not necessarily be valid for assessing the specific material taught in your child's class. Although reading comprehension may be tested, the reading passages will not come from the books your child is reading in class. Similarly, map reading or reference skills may be tested, but the items will not include the specific materials or topics covered in class. While these tests may be valid measures of basic skills, they will not necessarily be valid for assessing the degree to which your child mastered the particular material covered in, for example, a social studies unit on China or an English assignment on *Huckleberry Finn*. A teacher-made test would be more valid for that purpose. It is for this reason that you will often hear children complain that standardized tests didn't test what they were learning. Such complaints, however, do not necessarily bring into question the validity of the test, particularly a standardized test.

How can you tell if it's the validity of the test that's the problem? One clue is whether other children in the class are having similar problems. Is everyone complaining that the tests are unfair? Are there complaints that the teacher never covered the material on the test? This type of complaint from several youngsters does bring the validity of the test into question. In such instances, you might want to examine the test more closely. Ask why the test seems unfair. How did the test differ from what the teacher covered in class? Look closely at the questions. You don't have to be an expert to see if the questions seem to be trivial, tricky, or confusing. Do they require children to apply skills learned in the unit to novel situations, which may be perfectly valid? Or do they require students to know specific facts that weren't taught in class? The answers to these questions will give you some clues as to the source of the problem.

You can't, of course, assume that it is always the test that's at fault. Students sometimes complain about very good tests. Students who are accustomed to simply memorizing what the teacher said will often complain when a new teacher requires them to analyze material on their own, draw inferences, and support their opinions. If the purpose of the class is to develop these skills, however, a valid test will assess their ability in these areas. Looking at the test will help you understand what the test is testing and what the test scores represent.

As you can see, a test that is valid in one situation may not be valid in another, and the degree to which an achievement test is valid is dependent upon whether, in a particular testing situation, the test is measuring what you wish to measure. To fully understand what the scores on an achievement test are telling you about your child, you have to look at the content of the test in relation to the skills and knowledge you wish to measure.

APTITUDE TESTS: PREDICTIVE VALIDITY

Unlike achievement tests, which are used to assess current knowledge and ability, the purpose of aptitude tests is to predict future performance. For an aptitude test to be valid, then, we must have evidence that it does indeed predict the performance that we wish it to predict. A vocational aptitude test should predict how people will do in various work situations, and a scholastic aptitude test should predict how people will do in school. No matter how appropriate the content of the test appears to be, a test cannot be a valid aptitude test unless the test is a good predictor of the performance it purports to predict. The items on a test may seem totally irrelevant to the performance being predicted, but if the test is successful at predicting that performance, the test is still valid.

Consider again, for example, the practice of using tests of stamina, muscle strength, flexibility, and physical conditioning to select youngsters for a tennis team. Our first reaction may be to say it's ridiculous . . . and maybe it is. From the perspective of test validity, however, we would have to ask how effective these measures are in predicting performance on the team. If it was found that the scores on these tests did accurately predict the youngsters' performance in a series of tennis matches, we would have to conclude that, in fact, they were valid selection tests.

For an aptitude test to be valid, then, it need not have the same type of content validity that is required for an achievement test. It does not have to look as if it is measuring what we think it is. Regardless of what is included on the test items, an aptitude test is valid if it predicts the performance that it is supposed to predict. Aptitude tests that are predictive of future performance are said to have predictive validity.

The question, then, is how can we determine whether or not a test has predictive validity? Companies that develop and publish aptitude tests conduct validity studies in which they study the relationship between performance on the test and future performance in the area being predicted. They give the test to a large sample of individuals and then, after a period of time, examine how those individuals actually perform on the target task. For a scholastic aptitude test, for example, a testing company would test a large sample of students and then see whether those students who do well on the test are the same ones who, in the future, do well in school.

There is a number, a statistic called a correlation coefficient, that indicates the degree of relationship, or the correlation, between scores on the test and later performance in school. A correlation coefficient is a measure of the relationship between two sets of scores. It tells you whether those individuals who did well on the first measure are, in general, the same ones who do well on the second. For a scholastic aptitude test, for example, the correlation coefficient would indicate whether the students who scored well on the scholastic aptitude test were indeed those who subsequently had the highest grades in school. When correlation coefficients are used to determine how well a test predicts later performance, they are called predictive validity coefficients. They indicate how well the test scores predict that later performance. It isn't necessary to understand how the correlation coefficient is calculated in order to understand predictive validity. So much of our understanding of test scores is based upon the relationships among different measures, however, that it is important to understand what the correlation coefficient tells you.

Correlation coefficients are numbers that vary from a high of +1.00 to a low of −1.00. The correlation coefficient indicates the degree to which two sets of scores are related. When two sets of scores are highly related, the correlation coefficient will have a value close to either +1.00 or −1.00; when two sets of scores are not related, the correlation coefficient will have a value close to 0.00.

When the correlation coefficient is equal to +1.00, it means that the scores are related in such a way that individuals have exactly the same relative standing on the two sets of scores. Referring to Figure 2.1, for example, we can see that in the example where the correlation coefficient is equal to +1.00, the highest scorer on the test of musical aptitude also received the highest grade in musical performance, the second highest scorer on the test received the second highest performance grade, and so forth. A correlation coefficient of +1.00, then, would indicate a relationship in which high scores on the test were related to high grades in performance and low scores on the test were related to low grades in performance.

We call a correlation coefficient of +1.00 a perfect positive correlation. It is called a perfect positive correlation because, when the correlation coefficient is +1.00, knowing a person's score on one measure enables us to determine the score on the second measure *with perfect accuracy*. There is a perfect correspondence between each individual's rank on each of the measures.

To illustrate this concept, look at the example in Figure 2.1 where the correlation coefficient is +1.00. As you can see, each student's musical

Figure 2.1
The Relationship Reflected by Different Correlation Coefficients

A. The relationship between musical
   aptitude test scores and grades
   in performance when

	The correlation = +1.0		The correlation = +.88		The correlation = +.31	
	Musical	Musical	Musical	Musical	Musical	Musical
	Aptitude	Performance	Aptitude	Performance	Aptitude	Performance
Student	Score	Grade	Score	Grade	Score	Grade
Allison	10	10	10	10	10	7
Brian	9	9	9	7	9	5
Carlos	8	8	8	8	8	3
Deborah	7	7	7	9	7	9
Elena	6	6	6	6	6	10
Frank	5	5	5	4	5	8
Greta	4	4	4	3	4	1
Harvey	3	3	3	2	3	2
Ivan	2	2	2	5	2	6
Jessica	1	1	1	1	1	4

B. The relationship between ratings of
   hyperactivity and the ability to do
   quiet desk work when

	The correlation = -1.0		The correlation = -.88		The correlation = -.31	
		Desk		Desk		Desk
	Hyperactivity	Work	Hyperactivity	Work	Hyperactivity	Work
Student	Rating	Rating	Rating	Rating	Rating	Rating
Allison	10	1	10	1	10	4
Brian	9	2	9	5	9	6
Carlos	8	3	8	2	8	2
Deborah	7	4	7	3	7	1
Elena	6	5	6	4	6	8
Frank	5	6	5	6	5	10
Greta	4	7	4	9	4	9
Harvey	3	8	3	8	3	3
Ivan	2	9	2	7	2	5
Jessica	1	10	1	10	1	7

C. The relationship between scores on a test of muscle strength
   and a language achievement test where the correlation = -.01

| | Muscle | Language |
| | Strength | Achievement |
Student	Score	Score
Allison	10	6
Brian	9	1
Carlos	8	7
Deborah	7	9
Elena	6	2
Frank	5	8
Greta	4	10
Harvey	3	3
Ivan	2	4
Jessica	1	5

aptitude test score was exactly the same as that student's performance grade. Now cover up the performance grades with your hand. Knowing that the correlation was +1.00 between aptitude test scores and performance grades, and knowing that this correlation coefficient indicated a relationship in which everyone had exactly the same score on each of the measures, you don't have to see the musical performance grades to specify a student's grade with perfect accuracy. Since there is a perfect correspondence between the scores on the two measures, knowing that Brian had a score of 9 on the musical aptitude test enables you to specify with perfect accuracy that he also had a performance rating of 9. Similarly, if you know that Greta had a score of 4 on the aptitude test, you don't have to look at the performance grades to know that she also had a musical performance rating of 4.

In this case, if the musical aptitude test scores were being used for selecting students for a special program in performance, this correlation coefficient would indicate that the test was indeed a very good predictor of musical performance. We would say that, for this group of youngsters, the test had high predictive validity for the identification of performance talent.

By the same token, a correlation coefficient of −1.00 is referred to as a perfect negative correlation. A correlation coefficient of −1.00 indicates the same high degree of association, the same degree of predictability, as a correlation coefficient of +1.00, but the relationship between the two scores is reversed. In this case, there is a perfect negative correspondence between each individual's scores on each of the measures. Consider, for example, the correlation of −1.00 illustrated in Figure 2.1 between scores on a test of hyperactivity and teachers' ratings of students' ability to work quietly at their desks. In this situation, the correlation of −1.00 would mean that the student who had the *highest* score on the test of hyperactivity was rated as *least* able to work quietly at a desk and, similarly, that the student with the *lowest* score on the test of hyperactivity was judged to be *most able* to work quietly. In other words, in contrast to a perfect positive correlation, in which high scores on one of the measures are associated with high scores on the other, a perfect negative relationship is one in which high scores on one of the measures are associated with low scores on the other. The degree of association is equally strong, however, regardless of whether the correlation is +1.00 or −1.00. The only difference is that in the positive relationship, high scores on one of the measures are associated with high scores on the other and, in the negative relationship, high scores on one of the measures are associated with low scores on the other.

If you refer again to Figure 2.1, you can see that, with a correlation coefficient of –1.00, you can still use one set of scores to make perfectly accurate predictions of an individual's standing on the second set of scores. Knowing that the correlation coefficient is –1.00 between ratings of hyperactivity and ratings of a child's ability to do quiet desk work, you don't have to see the desk work ratings to know that, if Jessica's hyperactivity score was 1, she received a rating of 10 in her ability to work quietly at her desk. Similarly, Carlos's hyperactivity rating of 8 tells you that he had a rating of 3 in his ability to work quietly at his desk. Again, these data indicate that the hyperactivity scale has high predictive validity for identifying a child's ability to do quiet desk work.

In real life, however, we never find perfect correlations, either positive or negative, between test scores and future performance. For most of the better aptitude tests that are used in the schools, the values of the correlation coefficient tend to fall somewhere between +.70 and +.95. Consider, for example, a test of scholastic aptitude that has a correlation of +.91 with students' grades in school. Knowing that the correlation coefficient is +.91 would tell us that the scores on the test are not perfectly correlated with grades in school, that we cannot predict students' grades from their performance on the test with perfect accuracy. Nevertheless, the correlation is sufficiently close to +1.00 that we can say that, in general, students who did well on the test are likely to have high grades.

Similarly, in Figure 2.1, you can see that where the correlation is +.88 between musical aptitude test scores and musical performance grades, there is still a describable relationship between the scores on the two measures. We can say that, *in general*, those students who did well on the musical aptitude test received high performance grades, but the relationship is no longer perfect. Ivan, for example, did relatively better in his performance grade than he did on the test while Brian, who had the second highest score on the test, had a performance grade of only 7. With the type of relationship described by a correlation coefficient of +.88, knowing someone's aptitude test score does not tell you his or her exact performance grade. With a correlation of +.88, however, you would not be terribly wrong if you said that students who did well on the test tended to do well in performance and those who did poorly on the test tended to do poorly in performance. You would describe the relationship as a strong, but not perfect, positive relationship.

Similarly, a correlation coefficient of –.88 would indicate a strong negative relationship. Referring to Figure 2.1 again, you can see that, with a correlation of –.88, low scores on hyperactivity tend to be associated with high scores on the ability to do quiet desk work. Knowing a child's hyperactivity rating does not enable you to exactly specify that child's desk work rating, but it does give you a general idea of whether the rating is likely to be high or low. As the correlation goes down to either +.3 or −.3, however, you can see that the relationship deteriorates.

With a correlation coefficient in this range, knowing a person's score on one of the measures does not give you much information about that person's performance on the second measure. Look at the situation in Figure 2.1 where the correlation between musical aptitude test scores and performance is +.31. In this instance, knowing a child's test score tells you very little about that child's performance rating. Although most of those whose test scores fell in the upper half of the group also had performance ratings in the upper half of the group, Carlos, with a test score of 8, had a performance rating of only 3. In this case, we would have to conclude that the musical aptitude test scores did not have much predictive validity for identifying performance talent. The test scores provide only marginal help in identifying those youngsters who perform well and, if we assumed that the students' performance ratings would be the same as their test scores, we would be wrong in every instance. In many cases we would be wrong by a substantial amount.

As may also be noted in Figure 2.1, the same difficulties would arise if we were making predictions with a correlation coefficient of −.31. Although most of the students with high hyperactivity ratings had desk work ratings in the lower half of the class, we would make substantial errors if we used the hyperactivity scores to predict the desk work ratings. There is a very weak relationship between the two sets of scores, and using the hyperactivity scores to predict desk work ratings would be only minimally helpful.

The least degree of relationship is represented by a correlation coefficient of 0.00. In this case, we would know that there was no relationship between our two sets of scores. Referring again to Figure 2.1, you can see that where the correlation was −0.01, the youngsters who did well on the test of muscle strength had language achievement scores that were spread out from low to high. Knowing that a student did well on the muscle strength test tells us nothing about that student's language achievement; we would have to say that there was no relationship between muscle strength and language achievement and would conclude that the muscle strength test was not valid as a predictor of language achievement.

As you can see, the correlation coefficient is a statistic that we can use in assessing the predictive validity of an aptitude test. The closer the correlation is to either +1.00 or −1.00, the greater the validity of the test in predicting the criterion performance. The closer the correlation is to 0.00, the lower the validity of the test as a predictor. When the correlation is used in this manner, as an indicator of the predictive validity of an aptitude test, it is referred to as a validity coefficient.

When we wish to determine whether an aptitude test is valid, we have a number that we can evaluate in making this decision. The validity coefficient itself, however, is not quite sufficient to indicate whether or not the test is a good predictor of the performance in which we are interested. The validity coefficient tells us the degree to which the scores on the test are related to a particular measure of future performance, but it doesn't tell us the appropriateness of the measure of performance.

Assume again that we had a scholastic aptitude test for which the validity coefficient was +.91, and that this validity coefficient represented the correlation between scores on the test and scores on an achievement test taken three years later. What would this coefficient tell you? It would tell you that scores on the scholastic aptitude test were indeed predictive of later achievement test scores. Those students who did well on the test tended also to do well on the achievement test. But could you then say that scores on the test were good predictors of school performance? Not necessarily!

In this situation, although the high predictive validity coefficient indicates that scores on the scholastic aptitude test do predict achievement test performance, it does *not* indicate whether or not achievement test performance is related to classroom performance. In fact, we often find that performance on one test is related to performance on another test even when the tests are measuring different traits. This relationship occurs because, even though the tests may be measuring different traits, there are certain test-taking skills that would enhance performance on either test. We know, for example, that scholastic aptitude tests are better predictors of performance on achievement tests than they are of grades in school. Why is this? It is because many of the same test-taking skills are related to performance on both aptitude and achievement tests, while performance in class involves many other traits, such as diligence, responsibility, and cooperative behavior, that are not measured on either type of test.

The real question is whether in fact the achievement test scores that were predicted are an appropriate measure of school performance. As is the case with the assessment of content validity, there is no number which can be calculated to answer this question. The answer to this question comes back to a matter of judgment. In order to assess the predictive validity of an aptitude test, we must consider both the predictive validity coefficient, which tells us how well scores on the test predict a future measure of performance, and the degree to which that future measure of performance is an appropriate measure of what it is that we wish to predict.

Even if all the evidence indicates that a test has high validity for predicting what we want to predict, however, we have to remember that it may not be predictive for every child. Consider, for example, a reading readiness test given in kindergarten that is highly predictive of first-graders' success in an accelerated reading program. Even if the validity coefficient were +.95, it would not tell us that every child who performed poorly on the test would perform poorly in the program or that every child who performed well on the test would perform well in the program. It would tell us that, *for the most part*, a child's relative performance in the program is likely to be similar to her or his relative performance on the test. Nevertheless, the prediction for a particular child may be in error.

When a testing company does a predictive validity study, they find the correlation between the scores on the test and a measure of future performance for a particular sample of students. They then report the correlation coefficient that they find as their predictive validity coefficient. If it is high, and if the sample included youngsters similar to those to whom we are now giving the test, we can assume that, in general, the test will give us fairly good predictions of our youngsters' performance. Regardless of how high the correlation coefficient may be, however, it does not tell us whether or not a particular youngster's score will be predictive of that particular youngster's later performance. A high predictive validity coefficient indicates that the test will provide good prediction across large groups of students; it does not tell us, however, whether the prediction will be valid for any particular child.

Beth's mother, for example, may have given birth to twins a week before the test and Beth may have done poorly on the test because she was preoccupied with her feelings about her two new siblings. By first grade, however, Beth may have adapted to the situation at home and may do very well in the reading program. In other cases, there may be more subtle reasons for a test not to be predictive for a particular child or, perhaps, for a particular group of children. It is impossible to identify all the reasons why a prediction might be wrong for a particular child. When test scores are being used for making decisions about a particular child, however, it can't be stressed enough that the score should be evaluated in conjunction with everything else we know about the child.

Information about the predictive validity of the test tells us something about how much error there is likely to be in our predictions for a large number of individuals. There will be fewer errors if we use a test with a high validity coefficient, but not all errors will be eliminated. We have no way of accurately determining for which child the predictions will be wrong. We do know, however, that the faith we put in the test score should be tempered by how well that score fits with all the other information that we know about the child.

TESTS OF TRAITS OR INTERESTS:
CONSTRUCT VALIDITY

There are times when we want to assess traits or interests as opposed to school performance. We might want to identify children with test anxiety, for example, or examine a child's career interests. Tests for these purposes must also show evidence of validity. The way in which we assess the validity of tests of traits and interests is very similar to the way in which we assess the validity of aptitude tests. In both cases we look at the correlation between scores on the test and scores on another measure. In assessing the validity of tests of traits and interests, however, the other measure is not administered sometime off in the future. Instead, the scores are compared to scores on another measure that presumably measures the same trait.

Consider, for example, a test of anxiety. Assume that a school psychologist has developed a short paper-and-pencil test that she believes will help in identifying those youngsters whose test performance is diminished because of a high degree of test anxiety. How would the psychologist know whether her test really was measuring test anxiety? In other words, how could she find out whether her test was a valid measure of test anxiety? To answer this question, she would have to find out whether or not the scores on her test anxiety scale were related to other valid measures of test anxiety. She could, for example, have an outside psychologist come in and diagnose the test anxiety displayed by each child. Or she could have the children, or their parents or teachers, fill out a questionnaire describing how they felt about taking tests. Then, she could see whether those youngsters who get high scores on her test anxiety scale are the ones identified as highly test-anxious by the other methods. In other words, she would look at the correlation between the scores on her test of test anxiety and the scores on test anxiety obtained by other means.

In this case, the correlation coefficient would be called a construct validity coefficient and would be an index of the degree to which the test was valid. As with the predictive validity coefficient, however, a high construct validity coefficient alone does not guarantee that the test is valid. It is also important to determine whether the other measures that were correlated with the test scores are meaningful and valid measures of the trait being assessed.

Consider, for example, a measure of test anxiety. Knowing that there was a high correlation between scores on the test and a psychologist's diagnoses of test anxiety would seem to provide some evidence that the test was in fact assessing text anxiety. A psychologist's diagnoses of test anxiety is another meaningful measure of this trait; one would expect scores on a test anxiety scale to be correlated with a psychologist's diagnoses of the same trait. This correlation would provide evidence that the test is in fact measuring test anxiety. Suppose, however, that the construct validity coefficient reflected the correlation between scores on the anxiety test and scores on a scale of school satisfaction. A high correlation with scores on a scale of school satisfaction doesn't tell you whether the test is really measuring test anxiety. It doesn't matter how high the correlation coefficient is. If it doesn't represent the correlation between scores on the test and scores on another meaningful measure of test anxiety, it doesn't tell you whether the test is a valid measure of test anxiety.

To evaluate the construct validity of a test, then, you want to assess the value of the construct validity coefficient as well as the appropriateness or validity of the other measure or measures with which the test scores are correlated. As with predictive validity, however, there is no number that can tell you how valid those other measures are. That issue is a matter of judgment.

As you can see, tests are used for a variety of purposes, and different tests are appropriate for different situations. It doesn't make sense to say that a test is valid in the abstract. In assessing a particular trait in a particular situation, it is important to know whether the test has been shown to be valid for the particular use to which it is being put. A test that has high validity as a predictor of future academic success may not be valid for assessing mastery of a particular classroom unit. Similarly, a test that is valid as a predictor of scholastic achievement may not necessarily be a valid measure of intelligence, even though many of these tests are often referred to as intelligence or IQ tests.

As a parent or an educator, you are not likely to be called upon to determine a validity coefficient. Your understanding of validity becomes important, however, when a suspect test score is being used as the basis for important decisions about a child. Consider, for example, a child who is denied admission to an accelerated mathematics program on the basis of a single low score on a mathematics aptitude test. If the child has always performed well in mathematics in the past, you would have reason to question the validity of the score. The score on any test should be considered within the context of everything else you know about the child. In this case, if the child has never shown particular strength in mathematics, does reasonably well in mathematics but has never been outstanding in the subject, and has to be pushed to finish his mathematics homework, you would likely have little basis for questioning the test. If, on the other hand, you have a young woman who has a keen interest in mathematics, spends her spare time solving mathematical problems and has always been recognized as an outstanding student in this area, you would certainly have a basis for questioning the validity of the test as a predictor of success in mathematics.

Most school administrators want to adopt fair procedures for selecting students for special programs. They do not want to be seen as biased or as displaying favoritism. Consequently, they will usually be quite strict about adhering to the selection criteria that have been adopted for admission to a particular program. Those school districts that have more sophisticated selection criteria will usually have multiple criteria. That is, they will base their selection decisions on a variety of measures rather than on a single aptitude test. If, however, a particular test score seems to be at odds with the other information you have about a child, and the decision is based upon that test, you might wish to question its validity. Particularly if the test has a low validity coefficient, you would have a strong basis for questioning the soundness of the decision. You should remember, however, that even with a high validity coefficient, a test may not be valid for every youngster; a decision based on a single score that doesn't correspond with a child's usual level of performance is always open to question.

Our concern with validity, then, is twofold. Not only are we interested in knowing whether the test, as a whole, appears to measure what it was intended to measure but also whether it is equally valid for all youngsters to whom it is administered. In some cases, a test may not be valid for a particular youngster because of unique factors in that child's background. An English-speaking child from South Africa, for example, may do poorly on a social studies test because he or she is not familiar with the United States and simply does not have the background information that other children in the grade are assumed to have. Alternatively, poor performance may be due to a toothache, or an unusually high score may be attributed to cheating. Cases such as this do not necessarily bring into question the overall validity of the test. They emphasize the fact, however, that even tests that show evidence of validity are not infallible.

In other cases, there may be whole groups of youngsters who do poorly on a test because of factors that have nothing to do with their abilities or skill in the subject being tested. In these instances, we are dealing with what is referred to as test bias. It should be noted, however, that bias is not necessarily indicated by the fact that one group does better or worse than another on a particular test. If in fact the groups have different abilities in the area being tested, the test would not be biased, nor would the validity of the test be questionable. The problem of bias arises when the difference in the scores does not reflect a concomitant difference in ability.

Consider, for example, a scholastic aptitude test that is used to select students for an honors program in science. If girls get lower scores on the test than boys, this fact, in itself, would not necessarily mean that the test was biased against girls. It could very well be that because of other pressures in our society, the girls did not have as strong a background as the boys in science and mathematics and therefore did not do as well on the test. If, however, girls who performed more poorly on the test than boys did better in the honors science courses than boys, there would be evidence of bias. In other words, the test would be under-predicting the performance of the girls and would not be equally valid for boys and for girls. When such is the case, as it may be for different minority groups, steps should be taken to correct the bias. In some cases, the test should simply not be used; in others, scores may be evaluated differently for groups against which the test is found to be biased.

If you are interested in the validity of a particular test, there are several sources of information to which you may refer. For large-scale standardized tests, information about the validity of the test is usually provided in the test manual that accompanies the test. Test manuals will provide information, such as the validity coefficient for aptitude tests or tests of personality traits or attitudes, as well as the criteria with which the scores on the test were compared. The manuals will also provide information on what topics and skills are covered on achievement tests and the basis upon which the selection criteria were made. They may indicate, for example, that the arithmetic skills being tested were based on a review of second and third grade curricula in several states or that a panel of reading experts was consulted in constructing a reading readiness test. Often, test manuals will also provide information as to the performance of difference groups on the test, enabling one to assess the validity of the test for use with different segments of the population. Other sources of information on tests are educational journals that include test reviews, as well as books such as *Mental Measurements Yearbooks* and *Test Critiques*. More information on these sources is included in the appendix.

There is no outside source, however, that can indicate how valid an achievement test is for assessing a child's mastery of the content covered in a particular class. To assess the validity of a classroom test, the test itself must be examined in relation to the material covered in the class. The test will be valid to the extent that it parallels the course in both the subject matter covered and the skills required to respond to the test items.

We must remember, however, that validity is not the only issue we must consider in evaluating a test. The reliability of the test must also be appraised. An achievement test, for example, may appear to be valid—it may look as if it is assessing the subject matter it was designed to assess—but scores on the test will not reflect the extent to which children have mastered the material if the test is not also reliable. It is often said that a test cannot be valid if it is not reliable. This assertion, and the relationship between validity and reliability, will be examined in Chapter 3.

Chapter 3

Assessing Reliability:
Are the Test Scores Accurate?

Assume you were on a diet and were closely watching your weight. After two weeks of rigidly adhering to the prescribed menu, the day had come for you to weigh yourself. You woke up in the morning and, weighing yourself on the bathroom scale, were very pleased to see that you weighed only 122 pounds. You then had a light breakfast and decided to weigh yourself again. This time, however, much to your surprise, you weighed 115 pounds. You then got dressed and, being somewhat skeptical about that last reading on the scale, you decided to try again. You now weighed in at 150 pounds.

It's quite obvious that your weight could not have fluctuated to that extent in that short period of time. The scale must have been broken. The readings were clearly unreliable—they were inaccurate and in error.

Reliability refers to the accuracy of our scale values and, to the extent that the readings are inaccurate, we say that they are unreliable. A test is a measurement instrument in the same way as is your bathroom scale. Whereas your bathroom scale measures weight, however, tests measure knowledge, skills, interests, and abilities. In either type of instrument, differences in scale values should reflect real differences in the trait being measured. If the scale values do not correspond to your weight, but are erratic, they are neither valid nor reliable as measures of weight. The scale may look as if it is measuring weight, but it is measuring something else.

The "something else" that the scale is measuring is referred to as error and, to the extent that our measures reflect error rather than the trait we wish to measure, our measures are both unreliable and invalid.

MEASUREMENT ERROR

In testing, error refers to anything that affects a test score other than the person's true standing on the trait being assessed. The ideal situation is one in which every child gets the correct answer on every item on which he or she truly knows the information being tested and gets the wrong answer on every item on which he or she truly doesn't know the information being tested. Unfortunately, however, testing has not advanced to the point where this ideal can be met. Consequently, there are many times when youngsters incorrectly answer items that they really had the ability to answer correctly and correctly answer items that they really didn't know. In either situation there is measurement error. Measurement error occurs whenever a measurement instrument yields an incorrect measurement, regardless of whether the child's answer is right or wrong.

There are many sources of measurement error, but they can usually be sorted into one of the following three categories:

- Error due to the test itself
- Error due to the person taking the test
- Error due to the conditions of testing

Error due to the test itself refers to error that is caused by problems with the test. Ambiguous instructions, multiple-choice items for which there are no correct answers, or typing errors in a reading comprehension paragraph would illustrate this type of error. Were these possibilities to occur, they might lead to incorrect answers from youngsters who really knew the information being tested.

Similarly, a test that was constructed so that the correct answer could be easily guessed by youngsters who really didn't know the information would also lead to errors of measurement. In the latter case, however, the measurement error would lie in the fact that youngsters who didn't know the information were getting the item correct. In either case, we would have measurement error that was due to the test itself.

There are times, however, when error occurs because of other factors. When a child gets items wrong because she or he isn't feeling well and can't concentrate on the test, we have error attributable to the person taking the test. Or, if the examiner isn't paying attention and allows too much time on a timed examination, we have measurement error due to the testing situation. All of these types of error are referred to as measurement error; to the degree that error such as this affects performance on a test, it detracts from the reliability of the test scores.

Theoretically, test reliability refers to the degree to which test scores are free of measurement error. If there were no errors of measurement, then differences in youngsters' scores would be entirely attributable to differences in their ability, and the scores would be 100% error free. Tests are never entirely free of measurement error, however, and when we assess the reliability of a test, the goal is to determine the extent to which error contributes to the scores.

RELIABILITY COEFFICIENTS

In order to assess the reliability of a test, we have to have some way of estimating how much error there is in the scores. Although we can't directly measure the amount of error in a particular test score, there are various ways in which the reliability of the scores is estimated. The estimated reliability of a test is usually expressed as a correlation coefficient (see Chapter 2) and is referred to as a reliability coefficient.

In simplest terms, the reliability coefficient can be thought of as the correlation between children's scores on two testings with the same test. If the test were a true measure of each child's ability . . . and there were no error in the test . . . each youngster would be expected to get the same score twice. If this were the case, we would find a perfect correlation between the scores on the two testings, yielding a reliability coefficient of +1.00. If, on the other hand, the scores were affected by error, the error would lead to different scores on the two tests and the correlation would be closer to 0.00.

For purposes of illustration, let's consider an extreme example. Suppose a class of American high school students with no knowledge of Asian languages was given a test written in Chinese. If the students were instructed to circle the correct multiple-choice answer for each of the test items, they would obviously have no choice but to make wild guesses. Now suppose that two hours later they were given the test again. The second time, however, the order of the test items was changed. Some students might conceivably get the same score on both testings. Some might get the same score by chance; others might have systematically picked the same option for every test item. If one youngster circled option A, for example, for every question on each of the testings, that child would have the exact same score on both tests. If we eliminate those that systematically selected the same answer for every item, however, it is likely that most of the students had very different scores on the two tests. Their scores on each of the tests would be determined by error rather than their knowledge of the subject matter being tested. If we found the correlation between the scores on the two tests, it would be close to zero. Regardless of what the test was designed to measure, it would be measuring only error—blind guessing—in this scenario.

In real life, we assume that children will not be given tests in a language that they can't decipher. Nevertheless, they may be given tests that are too difficult for them, tests that cover work that they haven't yet learned in class, or tests that are so poorly written that they can't figure out what they are being asked. Situations such as these often lead to blind guessing and low test reliability. At other times, students may feel ill or may be distracted by other concerns or noisy test conditions. To the extent that factors such as these affect their scores, error is also present. If excessive error enters into the scores, the test will not be an accurate measure of whatever it was designed to measure. It will be neither reliable nor valid; it will be measuring error rather than the trait we wish to measure.

In estimating the reliability—and the extent to which error is present in the scores—there are three methods that are commonly used: (1) the parallel forms procedure, (2) the test-retest procedure, and (3) the split-half procedure. Each of these procedures yields a reliability coefficient.

Although the different reliability coefficients are similarly interpreted, it should be noted that the different reliability coefficients will yield different estimates of the reliability of the same test. The split-half procedure usually yields the highest estimate of the reliability, and the parallel forms procedure usually yields the lowest. For those of you who would like to more fully understand the differences among the different reliability estimates, a brief description is given below. The differences are not so large, however, that it is essential for a non-professional to differentiate among the different estimates. The important thing to know is that, in general, the higher the reliability coefficient, the more likely it is that the test is accurately measuring the child's ability. When the reliability coefficient is low, the error factors mentioned above are more likely to be present.

The Parallel Forms Reliability Coefficient

In determining the parallel forms reliability coefficient, which is sometimes referred to as an alternate forms reliability coefficient, the test maker constructs two parallel or equivalent forms of the test. Although the items on each form of the test are somewhat different, they assess the same content and objectives and are of equal difficulty. Then, a large number of youngsters take both forms of the test. It should be noted, however, that the two tests are not taken at the same time; they are usually administered several weeks apart. It is assumed that if, in fact, the tests were truly equivalent and were accurate measures of the child's ability, each child's score would be exactly the same on both forms of the test. The correlation between the scores on the two forms of the test is then determined and interpreted as explained in Chapter 2. If everyone had the same score on the two forms of the test, the correlation would be equal to +1.00. This ideal is never obtained but, the closer each child's scores on the two tests are to each other, the closer the correlation will be to +1.00. This correlation between the two forms of the test is called the parallel forms reliability coefficient. The closer this reliability coefficient is to +1.00, the more likely it is that the test is reliable; the closer it gets to 0.00, the more likely it is that scores are affected by error.

The Test-Retest Reliability Coefficient

The procedure for obtaining the test-retest reliability coefficient is very similar to the procedure used to obtain the parallel forms reliability estimate. Rather than having youngsters take two equivalent forms of a test, however, they take the same test on two different occasions. That is, the youngsters are retested with the same test.

The test-retest reliability coefficient is the correlation between the scores on the two testings. As in the parallel forms procedure, it is assumed that, if there were no error in the scores, the youngsters would have the same scores on both testings and the correlation between the scores would be equal to +1.00. In this instance the correlation between the two sets of scores is called the test-retest correlation coefficient and, again, the closer it is to +1.00, the more likely it is that the test is reliable.

The Split-Half Reliability Coefficient

In the split-half procedure, youngsters are tested only once. Then, the test is split into two halves: the even-numbered items form one half of the test, and the odd-numbered items form the other half. The test is constructed so that the even- and odd-numbered halves are of equivalent difficulty and the correlation between the youngster's score on the two halves of the test is obtained. This correlation is called the split-half reliability coefficient.

Again, if the test is an accurate measure of the youngster's ability, the score on the two halves of the test should be the same and the correlation should be equal to +1.00. The higher the correlation, the higher the estimate of the reliability.

Sometimes, when the reliability estimate is obtained from a single administration of a test, a Kuder-Richardson reliability coefficient or Cronbach's alpha will be reported instead of the split-half reliability coefficient. These coefficients are estimates of the split-half reliability coefficient but are obtained by using somewhat different procedures. The interpretation of these coefficients, however, is the same as for the split-half reliability coefficient. As with all reliability coefficients, the closer the value is to +1.00, the higher the estimate of the reliability of the test.

When interpreting any reliability coefficient, it is important to remember that none of them necessarily indicate the true reliability of the test. They are all only estimates of the reliability, and some of them yield better estimates than others. In comparing these different reliability estimates, the split-half procedure will usually yield a higher reliability coefficient for the same test than will either the test-retest procedure or the parallel forms procedure. The parallel forms coefficient will generally yield the lowest estimates. These differences reflect the different information obtained from the different procedures. Since the split-half reliability coefficient is based upon a single testing with the same test, it doesn't tell you anything about the stability of the scores over time. Only the parallel-forms and test-retest reliability coefficients provide this type of information. If, in fact, the scores are internally consistent, but not consistent over time, the split-half reliability coefficient will be highly inflated and not an accurate estimate of the stability of the scores. Thus, if you are using the reliability coefficient to compare the reliability of two tests, you must be sure that the same type of reliability coefficient is reported for each.

Although it is not likely that you will be called upon to calculate the reliability coefficient of a test, it is important to understand what these numbers tell you about the accuracy of the scores. The higher the reliability coefficient, the more accurate the scores are likely to be. But how high does it have to be for the test to be reliable?

How High Should the Reliability Coefficient Be?

There is no specific value of the reliability coefficient that represents a reliable test. Instead, you have to look at the value of the reliability coefficient in reference to a number of factors. These factors include both the type of test and the nature of the decisions for which the test will be used. Before we consider these factors, however, let's examine what the value of the reliability coefficient actually means. If you refer to Figure 2.1 in Chapter 2, you can see the relationship between sets of scores with different correlations. Look at the example where the correlation coefficient is +.31. If you compare the two sets of scores, you can see that there is very little relationship between them. Those students who did well on one of the measures did not all do well on the other. Assuming that a similar correlation coefficient was obtained when calculating the parallel forms or test-retest reliability coefficient, it would mean that, on a second testing with the same or an equivalent test, children's scores on the two tests would differ as much as they did in this example. In calculating a split-half reliability coefficient, this low a correlation would indicate that students differed to this extent in their performance on the different parts of the test. With that much of a difference, how much faith would you put in either score as an accurate indicator of a child's ability? A reliability correlation this low would indicate considerable fluctuation in a child's score. The child who scored at the top of the class on one testing might be just in the middle on another.

Which score is right? There is no way to tell from the scores. With a reliability coefficient this low, then, we must be very wary about concluding that the score obtained on any one administration of the test was accurate. In order to have a reasonable degree of confidence that the score provides an accurate assessment of a child's ability, you would want a reliability coefficient considerably higher than +.3. For use in making decisions about an individual child, you would hope to have tests with reliability coefficients of at least +.7. As may be noted in Figure 2.1, however, even with a reliability coefficient as high as +.88, there is fluctuation in the scores. With a reliability coefficient in this range, however, even though the scores on the two tests may not be exactly the same, students tend to perform at the same general level on both. Students who do well on one of the tests do well on the other, and students who do poorly on one of the tests do poorly on the other.

It would be desirable to have reliability coefficients as high as +.88 on all of our tests, but there are many tests for which this level is not attained. Achievement and aptitude tests, for example, tend to have higher reliability coefficients than do tests of personality or interests. Most of the widely used aptitude and achievement tests do not differ widely in reliability, and most do have respectable reliability coefficients in the range of +.75 to +.95. Tests of personality and interests tend to have lower reliability coefficients than do aptitude and achievement tests; the reliability coefficients on many of the personality and interest tests fall in the range of +.3 to +.5. It is very difficult to assess these traits and there is more error in the scores. With low reliability coefficients, we have less assurance that the scores will consistently fall in the same range. Of course, the low reliability coefficients may, in some instances, simply reflect the fact that people change over time. Nevertheless, when reliability coefficients are low we must put much less faith in the accuracy of the scores. The scores must be interpreted within the context of everything else we know about the child and should not be taken as the last word on a child's personal qualities or interests.

LENGTH OF THE TEST AND RELIABILITY

One of the most important factors affecting the reliability—and the reliability coefficient—obtained for a test is the length of the test. Consider, for example, a multiple-choice test with only a single item. If it happened to be on the one thing you didn't know in an area that you had really mastered, you would have a zero on the test. Or what if you misread the item? Or made a careless mistake and marked the wrong answer? You wouldn't really feel too comfortable with a one-item multiple-choice test, would you? You would want the examiner to look at a larger sample of your work. By looking at more than one item, there is more of an opportunity to represent your true ability. For essentially this reason, the reliability tends to be higher for longer tests.

Consequently, you should be particularly wary about scores on the smaller subtests of larger achievement or aptitude tests. Although the reliability of the total reading score or the total language arts score or the total arithmetic score may be relatively high, the reliability of the smaller subtests tends to be lower. When, for example, on an arithmetic test, there is one subsection on adding fractions and another on adding decimals, the reliability of those smaller subtests tends to be lower. Similarly, on a language arts test, the reliability of the total language arts score is likely to be more reliable than the reliability of the subsections on punctuation and capitalization. The reason for the lower reliability on the subtests is that they have fewer items, and one or two careless errors can have a marked impact on the score.

That is not to say that you should ignore the subtest scores, but that you should look a bit more closely at how many items were on the subtest and what it really means to get one or two items wrong. Again, this information has to be interpreted in light of everything else you know about the child. If the child generally does well in English and doesn't seem to have any problems with punctuation, a low score on a punctuation subtest may not reflect anything more than one or two careless errors on the test. That is not to say that a low score on a subtest should be ignored, but that scores on short subtests tend to be less reliable than those on the total test. When a score is unexpectedly high or low on a particular subtest, the assumption should not be that the score is necessarily more accurate than the other data you have. Discrepancies should always be investigated; you should be aware, however, that with a low reliability coefficient, the discrepancy may reflect error in the score.

ASSESSING GROUPS AND INDIVIDUALS

Other things being equal, it is always better to have a more reliable test. When assessing groups, the reliability does not have to be quite as high as would be desirable for assessing individuals. If you wanted to compare the performance of two classes, rather than two students, you could get an accurate assessment with a less reliable test. The reason is that, for classes, the error associated with each of the individual children tends to balance out. In other words, measurement error may lead some children's scores to be higher than they should be, but others will have scores that are lower than they should be. Over the class, these errors tend to cancel each other; we thus get a relatively accurate assessment for the group despite the error in individual students' scores. For an individual child, however, we have no way of knowing whether that child's score is accurate or whether it is higher or lower than it should be. We need a more reliable test where there will be less error in the individual scores.

THE STANDARD ERROR OF MEASUREMENT

Another way of looking at the reliability of a test is in terms of the amount of error that is associated with a particular child's score. The general relationship between reliability and error is such that the higher the reliability on the test, the less the error associated with a particular score. There is a measure, however, that estimates the number of score points by which a particular score is likely to be in error. This measure is called the standard error of measurement.

The standard error of measurement may be thought of as the average number of score points by which a child's score would vary if the child were tested with the same test an infinite number of times. Assume, for example, that Beth's knowledge of vocabulary was equivalent to a score of 80 on a particular vocabulary test. If the test were perfectly reliable—there was no measurement error—Beth would get every vocabulary word correct that she knew and every word incorrect that she didn't know, and she would receive a score of 80. Furthermore, assuming that she had no intervening opportunity to learn the words she didn't originally know, if we tested her over and over again, she would continue to get a score of 80 every time she was tested.

In real life, however, none of our tests are perfectly reliable—there is always some degree of measurement error. In the above example, then, if measurement error were present, Beth would not get a score of 80 every time she was tested. Sometimes she might carelessly miss words that she really knew, and other times she might make lucky guesses on some that she didn't know. On repeated testings, then, her scores would be somewhat different. The standard error of measurement would indicate the average amount by which those scores on the repeated testings differ from 80. The higher the reliability of the test, the less error there would be in her scores. The lower the reliability of the test, the more error there would be in her scores. The greater the error in her scores, the more her scores would fluctuate from 80 and the greater would be the standard error of measurement.

The standard error of measurement, then, tells us how much error to expect in an individual's score. It tells us by how much that person's score is likely to vary if tested at another time. Approximately 68% of the time, a child's score will be within one standard error of the child's true score, and 95% of the time it will be within two standard errors of the child's true score. Assume, for example, that Todd was tested on several occasions with a test on which his true score was equal to 75 and the standard error of measurement was equal to 5. We would expect that, approximately 68% of the time, his score would be within one standard error—or, in this case, 5 points—of 75. That is, 68% of the time, his score would be between 70 and 80. Similarly, we would expect that his score would be within 10 points of his true score of 75—between 65 and 85—approximately 95% of the time. When we see a child's score on a test, however, we never know whether the score reflects that child's actual standing on the trait being measured or whether it is at the high or low end of the fluctuations that would be expected to occur in that child's score. We never know, therefore, how far it is from that child's true score. As a general rule of thumb, however, we should assume that any score represents not just a single score value, but a range of possible scores that extend a standard error of measurement above and below the score obtained. Interpreting a score in this manner will enable us to get a better sense of the measurement error associated with any score.

If, for example, Michael had a score of 105 on an IQ test with a standard error of measurement of five points, we would conclude that his true score was probably somewhere between 100 and 110. Similarly, if Elena had a score of 107 on the same test, we would assume that her true score was somewhere between 102 and 112. As you can see, even though Elena had 2 points higher on the test, this difference does not necessarily mean that her true IQ score is higher than Michael's. Considering the standard error of measurement, it is possible that Michael's true score is actually higher than hers; Michael could have a true score of 108 while Elena's could be only 105. Taking the standard error of measurement into account, we can see that we should not interpret differences in scores as representing a real difference on the trait being measured unless the difference is at least one standard error of measurement. Even then, the difference may still be due to error. Interpreting scores in this manner, however, makes some provision for the error that is present in all test scores.

Reliability coefficients and the standard error of measurement will be provided for most of the tests published by large testing companies or developed by state departments of education. As you are well aware, however, judgments about a child's ability are not made solely on the basis of these types of tests. In fact, most children take many more teacher-made tests in the classroom than standardized tests. Most teachers, however, do not assess the reliability of the tests they prepare for their classes. That is not to say that teacher-made tests are not reliable. The problem is that the reliability of these tests is not usually assessed.

Understanding reliability can give you some insight into these tests, too. In the same way that standardized tests tend to increase in reliability as they increase in length, so too do teacher-made tests. That is not to say that teachers should use up valuable class time with many lengthy tests. Instead, a grade can be based upon a number of shorter tests, assignments and/or quizzes that, added together, provide a larger sample of a child's work. You would understandably be upset if a report card grade was based on a single ten-item arithmetic test or a single short essay. This unease would occur because you would intuitively realize how unreliable these measures are likely to be.

Even without any information on the reliability of teacher-made tests, however, you can suspect reliability problems when you constantly hear complaints about tricky items, confusing questions, and unfair grading. Most teachers do try to construct tests that accurately measure what they have taught; it is in their interest to have their students do well on their tests. Constructing good tests is not easy, however, and often takes a good deal of trial and error. If many children feel that the test items were confusing or the grading was unfair, it is advisable to review the test. It may be that the children have not really understood the work or don't really understand the requirements of the course. On the other hand, a review of the items may also indicate reliability problems: ambiguous or confusing questions where children knew the material but didn't realize what was being asked, vague essay examinations that could be interpreted in a variety of ways (only one of which was considered correct), confusing instructions, and so forth.

You should remember, though, that however reliable a test may be, none of our tests are perfect; even the most reliable of tests may not give an accurate assessment of a child's ability. The major question that both parents and teachers should ask is whether the score reflects the level of work that the child is doing in class. Whenever there is a marked disparity between classroom performance and test performance, it is appropriate to investigate why the disparity occurred. It is unfortunately the case, however, that parents, teachers, and school administrators often assume that the test score is revealing a truth about a child. Consequently, the test score is then used as the basis for decisions as to class placement or acceptance into special programs without consideration of whether or not the score is accurate.

How do you know that the score is accurate? You should always start by asking whether the score is consistent with the child's performance in school and on other tests. It would be unrealistic to expect a child to do exactly the same on every test but if, for example, a child usually gets a B in arithmetic, tends to do better than between 70% and 80% of the other children on the arithmetic tests given in class, and then does better than 75% of the other children on a standardized arithmetic achievement test, there would be no reason to question the accuracy of the achievement test score. If, on the other hand, you have a child who usually gets an A in arithmetic, has always performed in the top 1% or 2% of the class on arithmetic tests, and then scores better than only 75% of the children on the achievement test, there is reason to question the score.

That is not to say that the test is necessarily unreliable or that the score is wrong. It may well be that the child was absent for an important topic that was heavily weighted on the test or it may be that the child is having problems at home or social problems in school that are interfering with her schoolwork. On the other hand, it may also be that the child was not feeling well during the test or that she skipped an item and marked her subsequent answers in the wrong spaces on the answer sheet. The point is that a discrepancy does not necessarily tell that the test was unreliable; a discrepancy tells you that further investigation is warranted.

Another important point to remember is that no matter how high the reported reliability of a particular test may be, it may not yield a reliable score for a particular child at a particular time. If you see that a test score is at odds with other measures of the child's ability and that score is being used as the basis for making placement or other important educational decisions, do not hesitate to ask for a re-examination. Tests with high reported reliability coefficients tend to be accurate in making assessments of large groups of youngsters, but they may be wrong in the case of a single individual. Within large groups, the individual errors tend to cancel each other out—some students will score higher than they should have, but others will score lower. For that reason, tests are always more reliable when used for making assessments about groups as opposed to individuals.

Most teachers and school administrators are very much aware that none of our tests are either perfectly valid or perfectly reliable. They try not to use a single score as the criterion for acceptance into a program or for placement but rather look at multiple measures of the same ability. Even in college admissions decisions, where there is so much anxiety associated with scores on the *SAT* or *ACT Assessment* (*ACT*), colleges do not base their decisions on a single test score. We must remember that we use tests as simply one more source of information; none of our tests are without error and none can stand alone. They must be interpreted in conjunction with everything else that is known about a child. When a score seems out of line, you may certainly question the reliability of that score or the validity of the test. There may be, however, any number of reasons for the discrepancy.

In subsequent chapters we will look more closely at the different types of tests that children take in school. You may notice that we can put more faith in the validity and reliability of some types of tests than in others. That is not to say that we must reject those tests that have lower reliability. There are some very important traits that are difficult to measure. Rather than disregard those traits entirely and test only those things that are easy to measure, we temper our interpretations of the scores on less reliable tests. We must be aware that we can't blindly put our faith in a test score or allow others to assume that a test always gives the most accurate assessment of an ability.

Chapter 4

Achievement Tests: Measuring Current Knowledge and Ability

Consider a classroom unit on the American Revolution. The students learned about conditions in England, they did a project in which they impersonated the leaders of the Revolution, they read about Paul Revere's ride, they reenacted the Boston Tea Party, and they discussed the meaning of the Constitution. Then, the teacher gave a test to see how well they had learned the material covered in class: there were matching items in which they had to match people with places and dates with events, completion items in which they had to fill in the correct answer, and essays in which they had to explain the cause and effect of several important events. This type of test is probably the most common type of test given in school—it is a teacher-made achievement test.

The vast majority of the tests that children take in school are achievement tests. These tests are designed to assess the degree to which a child has mastered a particular skill or area of knowledge and may take the form of either a paper-and-pencil test or a performance test. Achievement tests include the classroom tests constructed by a teacher to test mastery of the work that was covered in a particular class as well as the standardized tests of basic skills that may be given to children all over the country.

Achievement tests may be further categorized as either mastery tests or norm-referenced tests. Mastery tests, which are also known as criterion-referenced tests, are designed to indicate how well a child has mastered a particular skill. The scores on these tests tell you how a child performed in reference to a predetermined criterion of mastery. A criterion of mastery is the minimum level of performance that a student must attain in order to be judged as having mastered the material being tested; all students who reach that minimum score are judged to have mastered the material regardless of how many others fall above or below the set criterion.

Norm-referenced tests, on the other hand, provide data—called norms—indicating how a representative sample of youngsters—called the norm group—performed on the test. The score on a norm-referenced test tells you how a child's performance on the test compared to the performance of these children. There is no criterion of mastery on a norm-referenced test. Rather, the child's ability to handle the material tested is assessed in reference to how the child's performance compared to the performance of the norm group.

The information that an achievement test yields about a child's performance depends upon the nature of the test. The information provided by a teacher-made test is different from that provided by a standardized test, and the information provided by a norm-referenced test is different from that provided by a criterion-referenced or mastery test. Nevertheless, all achievement tests are designed to measure current skills or knowledge. They assess a child's current knowledge, skills, and/or abilities and are not designed to necessarily be predictive of future achievement.

TEACHER-MADE VERSUS STANDARDIZED TESTS

By the time today's school children finish high school, most will have taken hundreds of classroom tests and a variety of standardized ones. Technically, standardized tests refer to tests that are given to all test-takers under standard conditions. For example, everyone taking a particular standardized test will be given the same instructions and will have the same amount of time in which to complete the test. Since most of these tests are published by large testing companies, however, standardized tests have come to refer to tests published by a company or agency outside of the school and administered to children in more than one school. Also characteristic of standardized tests is the availability of norms, or information regarding the typical performance of different types of students on the test.

One of the major differences between teacher-made and standardized tests, however, is the purpose for which they are given. Since standardized tests are usually published by large testing companies and are used by a variety of schools throughout the country, they must measure the knowledge and skills that are commonly taught in a variety of different schools. Although there are certainly some similarities in the curricula of the nation's schools, there are also many differences. Even in a course that may seem as straightforward as biology, different schools may give different weight to different topics and may use different laboratory exercises. Nevertheless, there is a common core of knowledge and skills that you would expect to be covered in any introductory high school biology course. Similarly, although the second grade mathematics curriculum may vary from state to state and from school to school, there are some common skills that you would expect all youngsters to learn regardless of where they are going to school. Since standardized tests are designed to be useful for a number of different schools, they are designed to measure that common core of knowledge and skills that one would expect to be taught in most schools.

Teacher-made tests, on the other hand, are designed to measure what was taught in a particular classroom. In a social studies class in San Francisco, for example, a teacher may use a unit on the history and geography of the city to teach not only factual information about the city, but also map reading and graph interpretation skills. When the teacher prepares a test on the unit, it would be appropriate to have questions both on the factual information that was taught regarding San Francisco as well as on the application of the map reading and graph interpretation skills that were taught. In contrast, a standardized test would focus on the general skills that one would expect to be taught in all cities and would not assess a student's knowledge about a particular city. That is not to say that standardized tests do not measure factual information but, rather, that they tend to measure information that one would expect most students to know rather than information that would be unique to the students in one locality.

Given these differences, it can be seen that teacher-made and standardized tests are used for different purposes. Teacher-made tests are used to assess how well a child has learned the material that was covered in a particular class. Report card grades and day-to-day instructional decisions are usually based on the results of teacher-made tests. Regardless of how well a child does on map reading skills on a standardized test, for example, the child's report card grade will not be high unless those skills are used to acquire the information taught in the classroom unit being graded. Similarly, although standardized arithmetic test scores may serve as a basis for assigning students to instructional groups in arithmetic at the beginning of the school year, or perhaps for placing some students in accelerated classes, it is the child's performance on classroom tests that will usually determine where the child stays.

The results of standardized tests are more often used for program evaluation and, in respect to individual students, for more general diagnostic, selection, and guidance decisions. Since standardized test publishers provide information on how students all over the country perform on their tests, school districts often use the results of standardized tests for evaluating how well their students did in comparison to the students in other districts.

If, for example, the students in one district compared favorably in all areas except for reading, that district might decide to look more closely at its reading program. Similarly, the results on a standardized arithmetic test would enable the school to identify students who are scoring below average in arithmetic skills. Standardized test scores are often used to assess student growth from year to year or to compare a youngster's relative achievement in different subject areas. Scores on these tests are often used as the basis for assigning remedial work or selecting students for accelerated classes; they are also used as a single yardstick on which to assess the knowledge of students from different districts.

Standardized test batteries such as the *Comprehensive Tests of Basic Skills* or the *Stanford Achievement Tests*, which include tests in a variety of subject areas, are used to assess relative performance in different subject areas. Different forms of these tests are often available for different grade levels, and the scores attained by a youngster in different grades may be used to assess educational growth. The *SAT II: Subject Tests* of the *Scholastic Assessment Tests*, which youngsters take in high school in such subjects as English, history, mathematics, foreign languages, and the sciences are achievement tests that colleges use to assess the comparative achievement of students from different high schools. The scores on the *SAT II: Subject Tests* are norm referenced, but some standardized achievement tests also provide criterion-referenced scores. The *Comprehensive Tests of Basic Skills*, for example, provide both norm-referenced and criterion-referenced scores in a number of subject areas for youngsters in elementary through high school, and tests such as the *College Board Advanced Placement Examinations* and the *New York State Regents Examinations* are standardized criterion-referenced examinations. The scores on these tests indicate the degree to which the knowledge and skills in a particular curriculum area have been mastered.

Achievement test scores, then, give parents and educators an idea of how a student compares to others or to a set criterion in respect to the common core of knowledge and abilities taught in most schools. Teacher-made and standardized tests are valid, however, for different purposes. Whereas standardized tests are geared to the more general skills that most children are expected to learn, most teacher-made tests, on the other hand, are mastery tests of the material taught in a particular class.

Furthermore, there are usually differences in the type of items included on the two kinds of tests. Most standardized tests have objective-type items—very often in the multiple-choice format, although other forms are also used, particularly on tests that are individually administered. Teacher-made tests, on the other hand, although they may also include multiple-choice items, tend to take other forms. It is on teacher-made tests that you are more likely to find essay items, fill-in items, true-false, and matching items. These item types differ not only in the nature of the abilities that they measure, but also in the reliability of the scores that they yield.

TYPES OF TEST ITEMS

Regardless of whether a test is a standardized test or a teacher-made test, a norm-referenced or a criterion-referenced test, the questions on the test can take many forms.

One major distinction that is made is between objective questions and essay-type questions. Objective items are those for which there is only one correct answer and, regardless of who is scoring the test, the score on the item will remain the same. Consider, for example, the following item:

The name of the first president of the United States was

    a. Abraham Lincoln
    b. George Washington
    c. Thomas Jefferson

There is only one correct answer to this question; regardless of who is scoring the test, anyone who selects George Washington as the answer will get the item correct, and anyone who doesn't select George Washington as the answer will get the item wrong.

With subjective items, however, the score will depend upon the judgment—or the subjectivity—of the person who does the scoring. Consider, for example, the following question:

Describe the current social, economic, and political conditions in the Middle East and describe how these conditions may facilitate or hinder a lasting peace in that area of the world.

In contrast to the multiple-choice item, where there is clearly only one correct answer to the question, there is no one right answer to this question. There will be as many different answers as there are examinees and, although some of the answers may have elements in common, no two answers will be exactly the same. Furthermore, the score that a student gets for an answer will depend on who does the scoring. Two teachers may not necessarily agree on how many points to assign to the same essay. As you can see, then, the score that a student receives will depend on who grades the paper.

Objective Test Items

Objective test items may take a variety of forms and may assess a wide variety of skills and knowledge. Consider, for example, the following items:

1. Draw a line from each state listed in Column A to its capital in Column B.

Column A	*Column B*
a. Arkansas	1. Albany
b. Colorado	2. Atlanta
c. Georgia	3. Augusta
d. Idaho	4. Bismarck
e. Iowa	5. Boise
f. New York	6. Concord
g. Minnesota	7. Denver
h. Oregon	8. Des Moines
i. South Dakota	9. Little Rock
j. Tennessee	10. Nashville
	11. Pierre
	12. Saint Paul
	13. Salem

2. If Mary had six marbles and lost two, and Johnny had three marbles and found another three, who ended up with more marbles? _____

3. Paw is to cat as

   a. Foot is to walking
   b. Toe is to ankle

c. Hand is to man
d. Milk is to cow

4. Write the last name of the man who was the Vice-President of the United States in 1983.

_____

5. Circle T if the following statement is true and F if it is false:

   We see lightning before we hear thunder because the speed of light is faster than the speed of sound.   T   F

Although all of these questions would be considered to be objective items, they differ in many respects. Items #1 and #4, for example, simply require the child to remember factual information. Note, however, that while the child must actually recall the information on his or her own in order to answer item #4 correctly, item #1 can be correctly answered simply by recognizing the correct city on the list provided. Quite obviously, it is easier to select the correct city from a list of cities than it would be to recall the capital of Idaho without being given any cues. If you don't believe it, ask a friend to give the capital of each state listed without looking at column B, and then compare the number of capitals correctly recalled with the number correct when your friend can select the correct capital from the list.

The difference between the above items, however, is not only in their form or in their difficulty. It is also in the thinking processes being assessed. Regardless of whether items #1 and #4 require recall or recognition, both items are assessing factual memory. Items #2 and #3, on the other hand, are measuring more complex thinking and problem-solving skills. These items also require some factual knowledge—the items could not be answered correctly by someone who didn't know the vocabulary or the number facts involved—but the correct answer requires much more than this factual knowledge. Although objective tests are often criticized for merely testing rote memory, you can see that these items are not limited to assessing the recall of factual information and may be used to measure a wide variety of complex thinking skills.

As you may have also noted, they may take several forms. Item #1 is a matching item, items #2 and #4 are completion items, item #3 is a multiple-choice item, and item #5 is a true-false item. In each case, however, the item is objective. That is, regardless of who might score the test, the same answers would result in the same score. There would be no argument among different scorers as to who was the vice-president in 1983 or who would have the most marbles. There is only one right answer to these questions, and that answer would be the same regardless of who scored the test.

Subjective Test Items

In contrast to the five objective items given above, consider again the question regarding the political and economic conditions in the Middle East. The answer to this question requires an essay, and the score received on the essay may vary depending upon who is doing the scoring. As opposed to the objective test questions, this question would be referred to as subjective.

Whereas a teacher's biases do not affect the scores on an objective test item, a teacher's biases and preconceptions about a student often do influence the scores on a subjective test. Although the teacher may take great care to be fair, a confused essay written by Andrew, who never seems to know the answers in class and is always fooling around, may be judged differently from the same confusion in an essay written by Jessica, who always seems to pay attention and to do her work correctly. Whereas, when reading Jessica's essay, the teacher is likely to read beyond her words and infer what Jessica meant to say, it is unlikely that Andrew would be given the same benefit of the doubt. These biases are human and cannot be totally eliminated. Thus, similar answers may result in different scores. In technical terms, objective items tend to be more reliable than subjective ones. Scorer bias is a major source of error in the scoring of subjective items, whereas this source of error does not enter into the score on an objective item.

Another problem with essay-type items is that it is often difficult to separate the writing skills involved in answering an essay from the subject matter being tested. Two students who are equally knowledgeable about the situation in the Mideast may get very different grades on the item noted above because one is more adept at writing than the other.

Essay tests are meant to assess writing ability to some extent, but the scorer should be quite clear about how much credit is to be allotted for the inclusion of the appropriate information and how much is to be allotted to the manner in which the material is presented. We all would like to see our children use proper grammar and spell correctly, but we would have to question the scoring of an essay where a child who has all the information receives minimal credit for the answer because of spelling or grammatical errors. It is extremely difficult to separate subject-matter knowledge from the ability to clearly express that knowledge in writing; this difficulty contributes to the error in grading essay examinations. In fact, good writers often prefer essay examinations precisely because they can use their writing ability to compensate for their lack of subject-matter knowledge.

Why, then, if essay tests are so problematical to score, are essay questions given so often on classroom tests? First of all, although they are more time-consuming to grade, many teachers find it easier to construct essay items than short-answer questions. It is very difficult to write good test items—both essay and short-answer items—and essay tests require much fewer items. More important, although objective items certainly do tend to be more reliable, they cannot assess how well a child can use the language, organize material, or present a logical argument. In other words, there are important learning objectives that simply cannot be validly assessed with objective tests. Essay-type questions are needed for measuring these outcomes.

Given the subjectivity of essay test scores, there are several steps that are often taken to improve their reliability. Although it is not always feasible to follow these steps, particularly on teacher-made tests, it is suggested that (1) more than one scorer grade each paper, (2) the papers be scored anonymously—that is, the scorer shouldn't know whose paper is being read, and (3) there be a model answer that indicates how credit should be allocated. Following these suggestions would reduce some of the bias that creeps into subjective scores and, in fact, these steps are usually followed when essays are included on major tests.

It should be noted, however, that even though there are questions regarding the reliability of subjective tests, objective test items are not always better. Good objective test items are not easy to write, and poor ones can be as unreliable as essay items. How many times have you seen true-false type items where the statement is neither clearly true nor clearly false, or where the words such as "never" or "always" give away the answer? Or what about completion items that are so open-ended that ten different answers are possible, and there is no clue as to what is expected. Multiple-choice items, when not well-written, are often difficult to read, and students who know the material can get the item wrong because they can't figure out what is being asked or because they are too rushed to read all of the options for each of the items. On the other hand, perhaps you remember taking a multiple-choice test where, even though you didn't know the material being tested, you were able to answer the item correctly because the options were written in such a way as to give away the answer. A good test item is one that is written so that all those who truly know the material get the answer right, while those who do not know the material get the item wrong. It is not that easy to reach this ideal, however, in either objective or subjective test items.

Performance Items

Not all tests, whether they be objective or subjective, need be paper-and-pencil tests. There are many areas where achievement is more appropriately assessed with a performance test. In physical education, for example, or in a typing class or a home economics or laboratory class, the measure of learning is not only whether a child can answer questions about what was learned, but whether the attainment of particular skills can be demonstrated. There is no way that you can assess a child's swimming ability with a paper-and-pencil test, nor will a perfect score on a written test indicate whether a child can sew a button on a shirt. For assessing skills such as these, it is necessary to use a performance test.

Some performance tests are objective, such as a typing test assessing the number of words than can be typed per minute or a swimming test measuring the time it takes to swim 50 meters. Just as with paper-and-pencil tests, however, performance tests may also be subjective. Consider, for example, the evaluation of a sculpture or of the form displayed in doing a gymnastics routine.

Just as with essay tests, there is more room for the scorer's bias to influence the score on a subjective performance test than there is on an objective performance test. In the same way, however, the choice as to which type of test to use depends on what it is that is being assessed. It is the issue of validity that must determine the nature of the test items. Whenever the trait or objective being measured can be measured objectively, an objective measure is preferred because of its greater reliability. In many instances, however, the important traits that we wish to measure simply cannot be assessed with objective measures.

Just as objective paper-and-pencil tests cannot be used to measure creative writing ability or the logical presentation of facts in the development of an argument, objective performance tests cannot be used to measure creative performance or the qualitative aspects of many skills. In general, you should be wary if only a paper-and-pencil test, rather than a performance assessment, is used to determine the level of achievement in a performance skill. Just as an objective grammar test can't indicate how well a child can write, a paper-and-pencil test about art or music or sports cannot tell you how well a child will perform in these areas. Also, given the scorer error that can't help but creep into the scores on subjective tests, you should expect more than one scorer to assess any subjective tests that are being used as the basis for major decisions regarding a child's future.

Just consider, for example, the number of judges scoring such events as figure skating or diving at the Olympics. And how many times is there agreement among all the judges on the quality of performance? You would find the same variation among judges of any performance and, where major decisions are based on subjective judgments of performance, the error or bias of each individual scorer should be balanced by the judgment of others. The same precautions taken to improve the reliability of any subjective test should be applied to subjective performance tests. Although it is desirable to use the most reliable tests available, the need for reliability must always be balanced against the requirement of validity. Where validity issues call for the use of a subjective test, however, every effort should be taken to maximize the reliability of the scores.

ASSESSING CLASSROOM PERFORMANCE

By far, the majority of tests taken in school are teacher-made achievement tests. They may be either objective or subjective, and may take the form of either paper-and-pencil or performance tests. Ideally, the form of the test will be determined by the curriculum objective being measured and the test will be fair, appropriately difficult, valid, and reliable.

Teachers are only human, however, and they do not have the resources of the large testing companies to assess the difficulty and appropriateness of all the tests they give. Furthermore, it often isn't until after the test is given and scored that the shortcomings of a test become apparent. It would be unrealistic to expect that every test a child takes in school will be a perfect assessment of that child's mastery of what was learned. Most of the tests given, however, should cover the material being taught, should not be tricky or picayune, should be neither too easy nor too difficult, and should be graded fairly.

In the lower grades, classroom assessment tends to be less formal and, aside from occasional standardized tests of aptitude and achievement, regular testing is likely to be limited to spelling tests and/or criterion-referenced progress tests provided by the publishers of the curriculum material being used in reading or mathematics. Although these progress tests are not teacher-made tests in the strict sense, they are designed for essentially the same purpose as teacher-made achievement tests. They are essentially mastery tests of the skills presented in a particular unit. On self-paced curricula, or curricula where children progress from unit to unit at their own rate of readiness, these tests indicate whether or not a child has mastered the skills of one unit well enough to go on to the next. These tests are constructed so as to measure very precise curriculum objectives.

In a reading curriculum, for example, there may be one test that assesses the ability to recognize words with the same initial sound, or another test that assesses the ability to identify words that rhyme. In a mathematics curriculum, there may be a test of the ability to add two single-digit numbers. These tests serve the same purpose as teacher-made tests in that they enable the teacher to assess the degree to which a child has mastered particular skills taught in the classroom.

In reviewing a child's performance on these tests, there are two questions you might ask. One question is how long it takes the child to master the sequential skills in comparison to the other children in the class. That is, how fast or slow is the child progressing as compared to other children in the same class? Second, as with any test, you would want to know whether the child's test performance is consistent with other indicators of that child's ability. Although formal classroom testing is relatively infrequent in the primary grades, there are a variety of informal assessments made by the teacher that provide information on a child's skills and abilities. This information should always be considered in conjunction with any test scores when assessing a child's educational development.

As children move on to the higher grades, there is likely to be an increase in classroom testing. The majority of tests will most likely be paper-and-pencil tests, although there will usually be a share of performance tests, too. You should expect to see essay tests in subjects where the teacher emphasizes the students' ability to organize material, develop arguments and express their thoughts clearly, and use the language effectively. In other subjects you are likely to see more short-answer tests.

The more information a teacher has about a student's mastery of the material taught, the more reliable the teacher's assessment will be. For that reason, it is preferable to have several tests and quizzes over the period of a course rather than a single examination. Just think of the anxiety that would be aroused in a course where the entire grade for the year is based upon a single final examination. As the number of separate assessments increases, the weight of each individual assessment decreases. Consequently, one bad performance will not be as detrimental to the overall assessment.

Tests, of course, are not the only means of assessing achievement, even in the upper grades. In most classes students are evaluated in a number of ways. When grades are determined, the teacher may consider such things as class participation, homework assignments, project work and out-of-class assignments, as well as test scores. Concern about the use of test scores has also been a factor in the recent trend toward portfolio assessment, where students compile a portfolio of representative work to be evaluated. Regardless of the mode of assessment, however, there should be more than one opportunity for students to display their abilities.

In assessing classroom performance, it is always important to look at the pattern of performance in reference to everything else you know about a child. On a series of sequential mastery tests in reading, for example, you might expect a child with language problems to progress at a slower than average rate. This same level of performance, however, would have a different meaning for a very verbal child who, in other classwork, showed evidence of having mastered the skills being tested.

Unusual performance on one test is not necessarily a cause for alarm. Any child can have a bad day, a day on which test performance is poor because of a headache or a stomachache or a preoccupation with other events. What you want to be alert for, however, is a pattern of inconsistency between test performance and other indicators of ability, unusual performance in one subject or on one type of test, or an overall decline in grades.

It would be unrealistic to expect a child to perform at exactly the same level in all subjects or even to maintain the exact same level of performance in one particular subject from year to year. In addition to the fact that grades themselves are not absolutely reliable indicators of achievement, you should expect that a child will have fluctuations in ability and interest from subject to subject and that some subjects will be more difficult than others.

The time to be concerned is when, for example, a child who has always been a top student in math starts to do poorly on math tests or a child who has always been a good student seems to be getting lower grades. There is no one answer as to why such discrepancies occur, but they can be indicative of an underlying problem. Sometimes it may be that a child is having difficulty in one particular subject. At other times, a discrepancy may indicate that the child is bored in class, is having problems with some of the other children, or is not paying attention to the task at hand. Discrepancies may also be indicative of learning disorders or poor skills in particular areas. A child may find the learning of a foreign language very difficult, for example, and may not do as well in that course as in other subjects. Or a sudden drop in performance in a subject in which a child has done well in the past may be due to a new teacher whose teaching style is not as comfortable for the child.

On the other hand, of course, the problem may be with the testing and grading practices. The tests may be too difficult for the level of the students. Too much weight may be put on spelling and punctuation as opposed to the information provided in an essay, or perhaps the questions are so vague that even children who know the information don't realize what is being asked for on the test. Objective test items may be poorly written: they may be ambiguous, there may be no one right answer on a multiple-choice test, or the items may be testing trivia rather than the important objectives of the course.

Teacher-made tests are not subjected to the same degree of scrutiny as standardized tests in terms of reliability and validity. Teachers use these tests in conjunction with an array of other information about each child in order to assess the child's progress toward mastering the material being taught. Teachers themselves will often make adjustments in their assessments when they find that test scores were not as they expected, and they will usually be alert to cases where performance is at odds with a student's other work. It is useful to remember that teacher-made tests should ideally provide information as to a child's achievement of particular curricular objectives and that classroom performance will not necessarily parallel standardized test performance. Although teacher-made and standardized tests do not necessarily test the same knowledge and skills, however, discrepancies between the level of performance on standardized tests and teacher-made tests deserve further consideration.

THE USE OF STANDARDIZED ACHIEVEMENT TESTS

Most school districts use a combination of teacher-made and standardized achievement tests for student and program assessment. Usually, the standardized tests will include both achievement and aptitude tests. Although classroom tests, particularly in the upper grades, may be given fairly frequently throughout the school year, standardized tests are usually not given that often. In some districts, a variety of different types of standardized tests may be given once a year; in others they may be given as infrequently as once every three or four years.

A school district may choose from a large variety of standardized achievement tests. These tests vary in terms of the subject matter that they address, the comprehensiveness with which they cover the material being tested, the grades for which they are appropriate, and the information they provide.

Some standardized achievement tests, such as those administered in New York State as part of the *Pupil Evaluation Program*, are developed and mandated by the state. Others, such as the *Comprehensive Tests of Basic Skills* or the *Stanford Achievement Tests*, are published by test publishing companies and are administered to the students at the option of the school district.

It would be impossible in a book this size to review every possible achievement test that a child may take. If you would like to read the reviews of a particular test, however, you may consult the *Mental Measurements Yearbooks*, or *Test Critiques*. Both of these books include reviews of a variety of tests and are usually available in university libraries as well as some of the larger public libraries. For now, however, let's just review some of the different types of standardized achievement tests that are available.

Achievement Tests in Separate Subject Areas

Standardized achievement tests are available for a variety of different subject areas. In the lower grades, separate achievement tests are most commonly used in reading and mathematics. At the high school level, however, standardized tests are available for most of the subject areas taught. Although some may be selected by the school district for use in guidance and placement, many of these tests are taken to gain admission to college or to receive advanced college placement in a particular subject.

Many achievement tests, such as the *Stanford Diagnostic Reading Test (SDRT)* or the *SAT II: Subject Tests*, are administered to many students at one time. Others, such as the *Woodcock Reading Mastery Tests–Revised (WRMT–R)*, must be individually administered to each student being tested. Group tests—those that are administered to many students at the same time—are the type normally used as part of the regular testing program of a school district, while individually administered tests are reserved for special situations. An individually administered test will often be given when there is reason to suspect that the scores on a group test do not accurately reflect a student's ability, when a child is known to have a problem that would interfere with test performance, or when a child is being referred for further testing because of problems in the classroom. Although group tests are much easier to administer, the advantage of the individually administered tests is that the person administering the test can see how the child approaches the questions and can thereby get a better sense of the factors affecting the score.

Many of the achievement tests in the various subject areas are diagnostic tests. These tests are designed not only to provide an overall index of the level of achievement in a particular subject area, but to indicate a student's specific strengths and weaknesses. Popular among these tests are the *California Diagnostic Mathematics Tests* and the *California Diagnostic Reading Tests*, the *Language Diagnostic Tests*, the *Mathematics Diagnostic Tests* and the *Reading Diagnostic Tests* of the *Metropolitan Achievement Tests*, and the *Stanford Diagnostic Mathematics Test* and the *Stanford Diagnostic Reading Test*. Many of the large achievement test batteries that include tests in a variety of subjects claim to provide diagnostic information as to a student's particular strengths and weaknesses, but one must be somewhat wary in interpreting the subtest scores on these tests. For a test to provide valuable diagnostic information—that is, to reliably identify particular strengths and weaknesses, the test must have a relatively large number of items on each skill being diagnosed. The major difference between a diagnostic test and an achievement battery is that the diagnostic test provides more intensive scrutiny of the component skills of the subject being tested.

Achievement Batteries

Many publishers of standardized tests provide test batteries, or a series of tests in different subject areas that are packaged together and have been normed on the same students. That is, the typical performance of the same students is used to assess a child's relative performance on each of the different tests in the battery. If a child has taken both an arithmetic and a reading test that are part of the same battery, performance on these two separate tests will be assessed in relation to the performance of the same group of children. The advantage of a test battery over individual tests in the different subject areas is that the use of a battery provides you with a single yardstick—the same norm group—to use in assessing a child's relative standing in several subject areas.

The *Comprehensive Tests of Basic Skills*, the *Iowa Tests of Basic Skills*, the *Iowa Tests of Educational Development*, the *Metropolitan Achievement Tests*, the *Sequential Tests of Educational Progress*, the *SRA Achievement Series*, and the *Stanford Achievement Test Series* are among the more popular achievement test batteries in current use. Some batteries, such as the *Comprehensive Tests of Basic Skills*, include different level tests that are appropriate over the entire grade range, from the primary grades through high school. Other batteries are more restricted. The *Iowa Tests of Educational Development*, for example, include only high-school level tests, while the *Metropolitan Achievement Tests* include tests for kindergarten through ninth grade. These batteries include tests in a variety of subject areas, usually including reading, mathematics, and language tests at all levels, with science, social studies, and reference skills often added in the higher grades, and pre-reading skills such as visual discrimination and letter recognition included in the primary grades. The tests included in these batteries are designed to measure the degree to which a child has learned the basic knowledge and skills that are taught in most schools.

To give you an idea of the types of items included on these tests, sample items from selected subtests of the *Comprehensive Tests of Basic Skills, 4th Edition*, are illustrated in Figure 4.1. The items are from forms of the tests given in the elementary school grades. In addition to the tests sampled, the *Comprehensive Tests of Basic Skills* also include tests of Sound Recognition and Word Analysis (in the early grades), Vocabulary, Spelling, Language Expression, and Mathematics Computation.

The Visual Recognition test assesses a child's ability to distinguish letters and match individual letters and letter groups. It is not necessary that the child recognize or decode the word; the instructions for this item are simply to fill in the circle under the group of letters that is the same as the group of letters in the box. The Comprehension test, on the other hand, measures the child's understanding of the passage; in order to select the correct answer, the child must comprehend the passage and the question. At this level, the Language Mechanics test assesses the application of the standard conventions of punctuation and capitalization. In the sample item, for example, the child must recognize that names are capitalized.

The Science test measures a student's general knowledge and understanding of concepts and methods of inquiry in plant and animal biology, ecology, matter, energy, earth, and space. The Social Studies test similarly assesses a student's general knowledge and understanding of concepts related to geography, economics, history, political science, sociology, and anthropology.

The Mathematics Concepts and Applications test measures problem-solving skills and the application of mathematical concepts. This test does not assess computation skills, which are addressed in the Mathematics Computation test. The Study Skills test measures a student's ability to find, interpret, and use information. In the sample item in Figure 4.1, for example, the student must use map-reading and interpretation skills to correctly answer the question.

As you can see, although the items address the kind of knowledge that a youngster is likely to learn in school, the knowledge and skills being tested are very general. The focus is not on information that is likely to be unique to one particular locale or curriculum, but on basic knowledge that we would expect all children to learn. In the social studies item, as in several of the science items not illustrated, the ability being tested is not the recall of specific factual information but, rather, the ability to interpret and/or make appropriate inferences from written material in the subject area tested.

On most of these tests, scores will be reported for a variety of different skills. When interpreting these scores, it is important to keep in mind that

Figure 4.1
Sample Items from the *Comprehensive Tests of Basic Skills, 4th Edition*

VISUAL RECOGNITION (Level K, Grades K.0 - K.9)

jam	pan	jar	pam	jam
	○	○	○	○

COMPREHENSION
(Level 12, Grades 1.6 - 3.2)

Larry walked from the hall into the kitchen. He stood by the table and looked out the window at a tree.

Where was Larry when he looked out the window?

○ in the hall

○ on the table

○ under the tree

○ in the kitchen

LANGUAGE MECHANICS
(Level 12, Grades 1.6 - 3.2)

I saw __(D)__ at the library.

D   ○ bob smith

○ bob Smith

○ Bob smith

○ Bob Smith

SCIENCE
(Level 13, Grades 2.6 - 4.2)

Which of these comes from a plant?

○ egg   ○ meat

○ milk   ○ apple

SOCIAL STUDIES
(Level 13, Grades 2.6 - 4.2)

What is a large body of salt water called?

○ a pond

○ a river

○ an ocean

○ an island

the scores on the shorter subtests tend to be less reliable than the total scores. Where there is a total language arts score as well as separate scores for such subskills as vocabulary, spelling, reading comprehension, punctuation, or word attack skills, the total language score is likely to be more reliable than the score on any of the subskills. Similarly, a total math score will be more reliable than subscores on such skills as math concepts, applications, or computation.

Figure 4.1 (continued)

MATHEMATICS CONCEPTS
AND APPLICATIONS
(Level 14, Grades 3.6 - 5.2)

STUDY SKILLS
(Level 14, Grades 3.6 - 5.2)

Which of these numbers is less than 50 and
greater than 30 ?

A   10

B   60

C   20

D   40

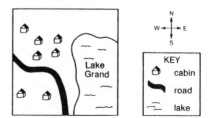

On which side of the lake are the
cabins located?

F   east

G   west

H   north

J   south

In fact, the subscores may be based upon very few items, and a difference
of just one or two more items correct can make a marked difference in the
score. Particularly when mastery scores are provided for discrete skills such
as punctuation, capitalization, or adding mixed numbers, they have to be
interpreted with great care. Although these scores can help to define a
student's particular strengths and weaknesses, it is very easy to "over-inter-
pret" these scores, that is, to assume that they provide definitive information
about a student's achievement. When there are very few items testing a
particular skill, however, one careless error or a good guess can make the
difference between mastery and non-mastery. These scores can be useful in
pinpointing strengths and/or weaknesses, but they should be used to supplement, rather than replace, other assessments of these skills.

Often when youngsters take standardized tests, they feel that they haven't
done well because they couldn't answer every question. Unlike classroom
tests, on which students are expected to get most of the items correct, most
standardized tests are designed so that it is very difficult to get a perfect
score. Norm-referenced tests are designed to discriminate among children
with different levels of achievement; that is, students who have mastered

the material to different levels of proficiency are expected to get different scores. If the test were too easy, students who had not mastered the material would get scores as high as those who had, and their problems would not be diagnosed. Testing companies put considerable effort into ensuring that their tests are at an appropriate level of difficulty, and the typical student should not be expected to be able to correctly answer every item.

On some tests, students are penalized for wrong answers. That is, not only do they not get credit for a wrong answer, but points are deducted. When such is the case, the instructions will indicate that there is a guessing correction, and students will be told not to blindly guess at items for which they have no idea of the correct answer. They will do better by leaving the answer out than by giving an incorrect response. If they have enough information to narrow down the options, however, it can be to their advantage to guess. This type of correction occurs most often in aptitude tests, and students should not be concerned about giving wrong answers unless they are given specific instructions to that effect. As in all tests, students should always be told to pay careful attention to the instructions.

When standardized tests are given, a number of different types of scores are likely to be reported. In addition to mastery scores for particular skills, you are likely to see such things as national or local percentiles, grade equivalent scores, raw scores, or stanines. All of these scores provide different information regarding a child's performance in the area being tested and are discussed more fully in Chapters 8 and 9.

Achievement Tests and Educational Decisions

The scores on standardized achievement tests can provide useful information on which to base decisions concerning a child's schooling. These test scores can point up areas of special strength, or they can detect areas where extra help is needed. They can give a teacher clues as to why a child may be having difficulty in some areas and can serve as tools in helping the teacher to assign a child to appropriate groups in reading or mathematics. In many schools, standardized achievement test scores also serve as one of the criteria used in placing children in accelerated or remedial classes, and the performance on these tests may also be used in deciding whether a child will receive remedial services from the school.

Remember, however, that test scores simply tell you how well a child performed on the particular tasks on which the child was tested at that particular time of testing. Wide variations are not uncommon and may be attributable to many causes. Perhaps the child wasn't feeling well on one of the testings, perhaps the teacher did (or did not) stress the particular content that was covered on the test, perhaps the third-grade curriculum in the child's school was very similar to that on which the test was based while the fourth grade curriculum was more experimental and didn't stress the type of questions asked on the test, or perhaps the child had a much stronger teacher in fourth grade than in fifth. Any of these factors could account for year-to-year variations in achievement test performance.

Additionally, it should also be noted that what sometimes appears to be a wide disparity in test scores may not be as wide as it seems. A difference of 20 percentile ranks may seem to be a significant drop in performance, but if that difference is between the 40th and 60th percentiles, it may not represent as much of a difference in performance as you may initially imagine. The interpretation of differences in norm-referenced scores will be discussed more fully in Chapter 9. For now, however, you should be aware that, with norm-referenced scores, large score differences sometimes reflect rather minor differences in performance.

The important point to remember is that a single achievement score is not necessarily any more valid than any other information that you have about a child. If the score on an achievement test seems at odds with the general level of a child's performance in class, it may be that the score is not a valid indicator of what the child has learned. The problems appear when teachers and parents assume that an achievement score supersedes all the other information that is available about a child. The score on an achievement test should be used in conjunction with the other information that you have, not in place of that other knowledge.

When achievement test scores are used to make decisions as to class groupings or placement in special classes, the important question to ask is whether the scores are consistent with the other information that you have. Does the placement seem reasonable, based on everything else that you know about a child? If the child has always been in the top reading group and continues to perform at the same high level in class, a low achievement score in reading does not necessarily mean that the child should be shifted to a lower group. The score should raise some questions, however. Did everyone in the class do poorly? How about the other classes in the school? Was the test testing the reading skills that were being stressed in class? Were there areas in which the child had particular difficulty? Are those areas going to be covered at a later time? Or is extra attention needed in some areas of skill development? The test score does not answer the questions but should raise them. It is the school's responsibility to find the answers, not just to uncritically use the test score.

On the other hand, if a child has not been performing well in class but does exceptionally well on an achievement test, there are other questions that you might want to raise. If the child has the skills necessary to perform well on the test, why aren't the skills being displayed in class? Are there other problems that are interfering? Is the child bored? Have there been similar disparities in other areas? Or was the test score just a fluke?

It should be understood that achievement tests do not necessarily measure the same material that is being assessed on classroom tests. Nevertheless, we can expect some degree of consistency between classroom performance and the performance on standardized achievement tests. Inconsistencies may serve as clues to problems that might otherwise not have been apparent, or they may just reflect a momentary lack of attention or a passing stomachache. Standardized achievement test scores may serve as an important aid in grouping students for instruction, or they may be used as a rigid barrier to finding the best placement for a child. Most of the most serious criticisms of testing are not of the tests themselves but of how they are used. The test scores can provide valuable information about a child, but it is the school's responsibility to make the best use of those scores.

Chapter 5

Aptitude Tests:
Predicting Future Performance

It's a rare college-bound high school junior who isn't concerned about the *Scholastic Assessment Tests* or, as they are more commonly known, the *SAT*. Most will probably tell you that they need high scores to be admitted to the college of their choice, but few understand exactly what the tests are designed to measure. The *SAT II: Subject Tests* are achievement tests as described in Chapter 4 but the *SAT I: Reasoning Test* is an aptitude test. Although performance on the *SAT I* is obviously related to the academic skills a student has acquired, the test is not another measure of achievement; it is not designed to see how well a student has mastered the subjects taught in high school but, rather, to predict a student's scholastic performance in college. The scores on the *SAT I* do not necessarily indicate who did best in high school; they predict who is most likely to succeed in college.

In contrast to achievement tests, which measure current ability and knowledge, aptitude tests are designed to predict future performance. In appearance, aptitude tests may look the same as achievement tests, but they differ in purpose. Whereas an achievement test must be composed of items that are representative of the content area being assessed, the only require-ment of the items on an aptitude test is that they predict a child's perform-ance on the trait being assessed. A scholastic aptitude test would be valid, or have predictive validity, if the scores on the test were good predictors of later school performance. Similarly, a foreign language aptitude test would have predictive validity if the scores on the test were good predictors of grades in subsequent foreign language courses, and a test of musical aptitude would have predictive validity if the scores on the test were good predictors of those who later displayed musical talent.

Unlike an achievement test, the items on an aptitude test may not necessarily appear to be measuring what it is that they are actually predicting. If, for example, it were true that only good students preferred cereal to eggs, preferred chocolate to vanilla ice cream, preferred the color yellow to the color red, preferred going to the circus to going on a picnic, and preferred the oboe to the piano, then a test that asked a child's preferences in these areas might have predictive validity as a scholastic aptitude test. You might look at the test and say that it was ridiculous. After all, the items seem to have nothing to do with school success. Nevertheless, if scores on the test were in fact effective predictors of school performance, the test would be said to have predictive validity. The major question that must be answered in evaluating an aptitude test is whether or not it predicts future performance. A fuller discussion of how to assess the predictive validity of an aptitude test appears in Chapter 2. In this chapter, the discussion will center on the different types of aptitude tests that are commonly used in the schools and the type of information that these tests provide.

SCHOLASTIC APTITUDE TESTS

Scholastic aptitude tests are tests that predict school performance. The previously described *SAT I: Reasoning Test* that is administered to high school students who are seeking college admission is a scholastic aptitude test because it is designed to predict college performance. This test is not the only type of scholastic aptitude test, however. It is likely that a child will have taken a number of other scholastic aptitude tests before reaching the upper high school grades. This category of tests includes readiness tests, tests predictive of performance in different subject areas, and the category of tests that are commonly referred to as IQ or intelligence tests. In some school districts, these tests are administered before a child even begins kindergarten. All of these tests are designed to predict future performance. It must be remembered, however, that none of these tests is perfect. As discussed in Chapter 2, no test is perfectly reliable, and none has a predictive validity coefficient of +1.00. Regardless of the type of performance being predicted, the higher the predictive validity coefficient of the test, the better the prediction is likely to be. In no case, however, can one score on one test be taken as an irrefutable predictor. It is for this reason that colleges use a combination of measures in arriving at admissions decisions; they consider not only aptitude test scores, but such factors as high school average, class rank, the reputation of the high school, the difficulty of the courses taken, references of teachers, and writing samples. Although these various measures are not strictly aptitude tests, decisions based on a combination of factors are more predictive of success in college than are those based on the score on a single aptitude test.

Readiness Tests

The first type of aptitude test that a child is likely to take is a readiness test. These tests are sometimes called prognostic tests; they are designed to assess whether a child has the skills necessary to learn a particular subject. In kindergarten, for example, a child may be given a reading readiness test to assess his or her readiness to begin formal reading instruction. Among the more popular reading readiness tests are the *Metropolitan Readiness Tests*, the *Lee-Clark Reading Readiness Test*, and the *Gates-MacGinitie Reading Readiness Skills* test. They typically test such skills as letter recognition, verbal comprehension, and the matching and discrimination of visual forms. The assumption behind these tests is that if a child does not have these prerequisite skills, the child will not be successful in a formal reading program.

To illustrate the type of items that are found on these tests, sample items from the *Metropolitan Readiness Tests* are included in Figure 5.1. The first four items in Figure 5.1 are from Level 1, which is designed for four-year-olds in the pre-school setting as well as for youngsters in the beginning to the middle of kindergarten. The sample Finding Patterns item is from Level 2, which is designed for use at the middle and end of kindergarten and the beginning of first grade. These tests measure the skills needed in beginning reading and mathematics.

For each item on the Beginning Consonants Test, the teacher identifies each of the pictures by name and then asks the child to fill in the circle under the picture that begins with the same initial sound as do two sample words. In the item illustrated, for example, the teacher says the following:

move your finger down to the row where you see a little MOON. The pictures in this row are CAT, SOCK, MILK, and ARM. Fill in the circle under the picture that begins with the same sound as CALL and CAME.

Figure 5.1
Sample Items from the *Metropolitan Readiness Tests: 5th Edition*

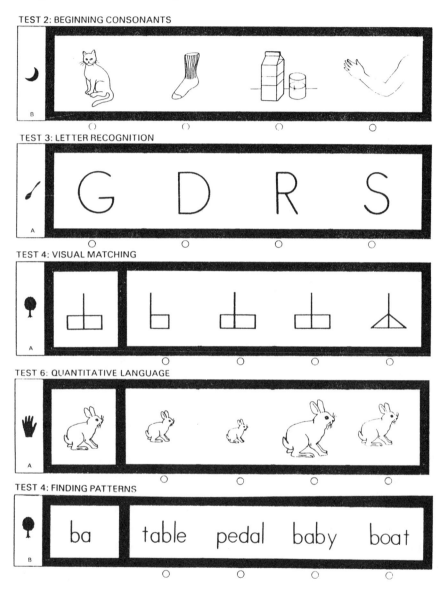

TEST 2: BEGINNING CONSONANTS

TEST 3: LETTER RECOGNITION

TEST 4: VISUAL MATCHING

TEST 6: QUANTITATIVE LANGUAGE

TEST 4: FINDING PATTERNS

For each of the items on the Letter Recognition Test, the teacher instructs the children to fill in the circle under a particular letter. In the sample item, the children are to identify the S. On the Visual Matching Test, the youngsters are instructed to indicate the box that contains the same shape as does the shaded box to the left. The Finding Patterns Test is similar to the Visual Matching Test. On this test, however, the item in the shaded box is embedded within a larger pattern. In the sample, the children must identify the group of letters that contains within it exactly the same sequence—ba—as in the shaded box.

The Quantitative Language Test assesses children's understanding of quantitative concepts such as "larger than" and "smaller than" as well as their ability to do simple quantitative operations. In the sample item from this test in Figure 5.1, for example, the children are instructed to mark the rabbit that is bigger than the rabbit in the shaded box. As you may see, the skills tested on these tests are those that one would expect a child to need in order to learn to read and do arithmetic.

Although readiness tests are useful in identifying youngsters who may need additional work before commencing with formal instruction in reading, their validity coefficients tend not to be very high. Cognitive development is uneven in this age group, and leaps in cognitive growth may occur over relatively short periods of time. Furthermore, even a child who has the cognitive ability to succeed in reading may not do well for other reasons. The child may not have the ability to sit still long enough for a formal lesson or may be too easily distracted.

If a child takes a reading readiness test, the scores should be taken as only one indicator of readiness for formal instruction. High scores do not necessarily indicate that the child will be a top reader but may be a sign of rapid early development. Similarly, low scores do not necessarily mean that the child will be a poor reader. Low scores may indicate that the child needs more readiness work or perhaps a little more time to mature. The children who learn to read the fastest in first grade are not necessarily the best readers by the time they finish high school.

The scores on these tests provide useful information that may help the teacher plan the most appropriate reading placement and/or program for a child. The scores can add to the teacher's understanding of the child's progress. They can support a teacher's assessment and can help in identifying problems. It must be remembered, however, that no aptitude test is 100% accurate in its predictions and that the scores must be interpreted within the context of everything else that is known about the child.

If the child has been making normal progress in pre-reading skills and does not have problems in his or her schoolwork, then low scores on a reading readiness test may not be valid for that child at that time. If the scores do not fit in with other indices of the child's ability, it cannot be assumed that the scores necessarily provide the most accurate assessment of the child's ability. Such a discrepancy is cause for further investigation. Was the child not feeling well when tested? Was something distracting happening at home? Were the instructions misunderstood? Or, perhaps, is the test revealing a previously unrecognized problem? The score doesn't answer these questions but indicates the need to raise them.

Although reading readiness tests are the most commonly administered readiness tests, readiness tests are also given in other areas. There are tests that assess readiness for formal arithmetic instruction, as well as tests such as the *Orleans-Hanna Algebra Prognosis Test*, that predict a student's likelihood of succeeding in algebra. Another subject in which readiness tests are administered is foreign language. The *Modern Language Aptitude Test*, for example, measures a student's likelihood of success in a foreign language course. Readiness tests such as these are used primarily to identify youngsters who may have difficulty in moving ahead in the subjects tested, but the scores on any such test can never be taken as an absolute indicator of how a child will perform. As on any test, a low score is not an absolute indication that a child will do poorly but a symptom that must be interpreted in view of other available information.

General School Aptitude and Intelligence Tests

Unlike readiness tests, which are designed to predict performance in one academic area and which measure skills associated with that particular area, the general school aptitude and intelligence tests attempt to measure those broader abilities that underlie school performance across a range of subjects. Rather than measuring information learned specifically in school, such as the names of the state capitals or the identification of different parts of speech, these tests assess general problem-solving and reasoning skills.

Some of these tests, IQ or intelligence tests, have been assumed to measure an immutable, innate ability. There is no basis for this assumption; regardless of how general the abilities are that these tests measure, all of these tests are, to some extent, dependent upon past learning both in and out of school. Performance on these tests, therefore, is dependent not only on a child's innate ability, but on the child's past educational experiences and opportunities for learning.

Furthermore, although some of these tests are referred to as intelligence tests, it is difficult to establish their validity as measures of intelligence. There is little agreement among psychologists or educators as to either the traits that should be included in measuring intelligence or the ways in which it should be measured, and there is much criticism that these tests measure only a very limited portion of one's intellectual skills. What these tests do measure, however, are skills that underlie success in school-related performance. Regardless of whether these abilities are learned or are innate, students who do well on these tests tend to do well in school, and those who do poorly on these tests tend to do poorly in school. Thus, regardless of whether or not they measure intelligence, they are scholastic aptitude tests.

When you think of these tests as scholastic aptitude tests rather than as intelligence tests, you are less likely to draw erroneous conclusions about the meaning of the scores. Many of these tests do yield an IQ score, or Intelligence Quotient, which is merely a score that indicates a child's performance on the test relative to other children of the same age. Although people tend to assume that an IQ is something that a child possesses, an unchanging characteristic such as blue eyes, left-handedness, or freckles, the IQ is simply a score on a test and may vary from test to test.

Originally, the IQ represented the quotient of the child's mental age, which was derived from test performance, divided by the child's chronological age and multiplied by 100. As may be seen in Figure 5.2, Martina, a 12-year-old who had a mental age of 12 as measured by the test, has an IQ of 100.

Ten-year-old Jill, who performed exactly the same as 12-year-old Martina on the test, had the same mental age of 12, but had an IQ of 120. As you can see, the IQ score is a relative measure that takes into account the level of the child's performance relative to the child's age. The same performance on the test will result in different IQ scores for youngsters of

Figure 5.2
The Intelligence Quotient

Name	Mental Age (MA)	Chronological Age (CA)	Intelligence Quotient $IQ = (\frac{MA}{CA}) \times 100$
Martina A.	12	12	$(\frac{12}{12}) \times 100 = 1 \times 100 = 100$
Jill B.	12	10	$(\frac{12}{10}) \times 100 = 1.2 \times 100 = 120$

different ages. A score of 100 indicates that the child is performing at the level typical of youngsters that age. Scores higher than 100 indicate above-average performance, and scores below 100 indicate performance below the average for the child's age group. Today, the IQ is no longer calculated as a quotient but still indicates the extent to which a particular child's score differs from the typical score of children of the same age. This score is referred to as a deviation IQ and, within a given age group, the average would be 100.

At this point, however, it is important to realize that the IQ, regardless of how it is calculated, represents a measure of relative performance on a particular test. The IQ is not an immutable characteristic of a child. It is unlikely that a child would score 140 on one IQ test and 85 on another a few weeks later, but changes do occur. When different tests are administered, the difference may be due to differences in the questions on the tests. Sometimes, the difference in scores on two IQ tests merely indicates that, on one of the tests, the child wasn't paying attention or wasn't feeling well. At other times, the difference may be due to real differences in ability. A child who has gone through a traumatic period may not be any less intelligent than at previous times, but may be easily distracted and unable to concentrate on learning. If tested in such a period, a child's score may go down, but may be a valid indicator of possible difficulty in learning. Similarly, there may be an increase in the IQ of a child from a disadvantaged home who is given enrichment opportunities. Can we say that the child has become more intelligent? That point may be argued, but it is likely that the increase in IQ score will be accompanied by better performance in school. In other words, regardless of whether or not these tests are measuring intelligence, they tend to be fairly valid predictors of school performance. It must be remembered, however, that they are not perfect predictors, nor are they equally predictive for all youngsters.

Predictions tend to be more accurate during the elementary school years and over shorter periods of time than in the high school grades or over longer periods. Infant and pre-school aptitude tests do exist, but their predictive validity is not high. Young children display different rates of development, and these early tests are often measures of a child's level of development. The child who shows a relatively high degree of eye-hand coordination as a two-year-old may have developed these skills at a faster rate than his or her peers. This early development does not necessarily mean that, as a ten-year-old, when many of the other children will have caught up, the child will still demonstrate above-average performance. There is much less growth between the ages of ten and twelve than there is between the ages of one and three, and it is more likely that a difference detected in the later age range represents a more enduring difference in the skill being assessed. Furthermore, many of the tasks that are measured on the early childhood tests are closely related to the child's level of physical development and do not necessarily correlate that highly with the cognitive tasks that are required of school children.

A scholastic aptitude test given in third grade is likely to measure many of the same skills that are needed for success in fourth grade and is much more likely to be predictive of fourth grade performance than would a test given at the age of two. Not only are the skills tested on a third grade test more directly related to the cognitive tasks required in school, but there is less time between the testing and the predicted performance during which events can occur that might modify school performance.

Even over the short run, however, it should be noted that two testings with the identical test will not necessarily yield identical scores and that aptitude test scores correlate more highly with achievement test scores than they do with measures of classroom performance. In other words, test performance on one type of test correlates more highly with test perform- ance on other types of tests than it does with the other behaviors associated with classroom performance. Even at the high school level, cumulative measures of classroom performance are better predictors of college grades than are aptitude test scores, although predictions are improved when a combination of both classroom performance and test performance is used as the basis of prediction.

Classroom performance, whether in elementary school, high school, or college, is dependent upon a variety of factors other than a child's level of ability. Particularly in the upper grades, factors such as motivation, dili- gence, and study skills are major determinants of grades. A child who is far above average in ability may not do well because of lack of motivation, while a very diligent student with lower aptitude test scores may do very well. Furthermore, it should also be remembered that some students simply do not test well, and their test scores are not indicative of the level of performance that they can attain.

Scholastic aptitude tests may take many forms. There are individually administered tests that do not require any reading on the part of the child, and there are group paper-and-pencil tests. There are tests that require the child to read the items, and there are those which are designed to be both culture- and language-free. These different types of tests are generally used for different purposes and have different advantages and drawbacks.

Group Tests of Scholastic Aptitude

Most school districts that administer scholastic aptitude tests as part of a regular testing program will use a test that can be administered to an entire class of students at one time. These tests are referred to as group tests and are usually administered by the classroom teacher in the regular classroom.

Among the currently popular group tests of scholastic aptitude are the *Cognitive Abilities Test*, the *Otis-Lennon School Ability Test*, the *School and College Ability Tests (SCAT)*, and the *Test of Cognitive Skills*. The *SAT I: Reasoning Test* is also a group test that is given to large numbers of high school students at the same time. These tests assess such areas as verbal and numerical reasoning, problem solving, and spatial relations. Most of these tests are paper-and-pencil tests, and answers are marked either in the test booklet or on a separate answer sheet. The teacher will read a standard set of instructions to the class and will give an example of how the test items are to be answered. In the lower grades, the teacher will also read the instructions for each item to the class. In the upper grades, however, most of these tests require the students to read each item and to select the correct answer from among those provided.

Typical of the questions on these tests are the sample items from the *Test of Cognitive Skills* illustrated in Figure 5.3. The Sequence items require the child to discern sequential patterns and, based on the patten, identify the next step in the sequence. For the item in the upper left, for example, the instructions are:

The figures in the top row are arranged in a certain order, forming a pattern. Try to see what the pattern is in this row of figures. Then look at the four answer choices in the bottom row. Find the one that would come next in the pattern.

The item in the upper right of Figure 5.3 similarly requires the child to find the pattern in the sequence of letters and to select the letter that would continue the pattern.

For the Analogies item, the child must determine how the dog and the doghouse in the top two boxes are related and then determine which of the answer choices is related to the automobile in the same way that the doghouse is related to the dog. In the Verbal Reasoning item about Big Ben, the child is required to determine which of the answer choices logically must be true if the premises are true. In the second item, the child must indicate which word in a series of words does not belong with the others.

Figure 5.3
Sample Items from the *Test of Cognitive Skills, 2nd Edition*

Sequences

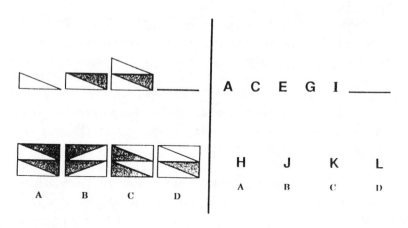

A   C   E   G   I ____

H   J   K   L

A   B   C   D

Analogies

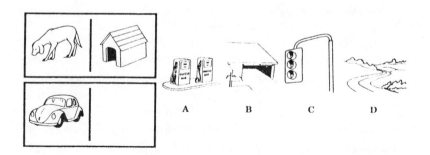

A   B   C   D

Verbal Reasoning

Big Ben is a clock in England.

Judy has visited Big Ben.   pond   lake   mountain   ocean

A   People often visit Big Ben.   A   B   C   D

B   Many clocks in England are big.

C   Big Ben is named after a person.

D   Judy has been to England.

As you can see, these items do not test the content knowledge learned in a particular course but, rather, more general thinking and problem-solving skills. Rather than testing the material taught in a particular course, these problems draw upon thinking skills developed from a variety of sources. In fact, it is very unlikely for problems such as these to be included on classroom tests designed to assess mastery of course material.

When administering a group test, the teacher is responsible for seeing that there is order in the classroom and for answering questions that are raised before the examination begins. The teacher is not able to follow the performance of each individual child in the class during the administration of the test, however, and may not correct misconceptions in the way a child marks the answers or explain the meaning of words that a child may not understand. If a child is not sure of what an item is asking, the only response a teacher may give is to tell the child to try his or her best. The teacher may not explain the item or tell the child how to figure it out. When the test has been scored, the teacher will learn the child's score on the test but not how the child arrived at the answers.

Particularly in the upper grades, reading ability is a major factor that may enter into the performance on these tests. Although the tests are designed so that the reading level of the test should not surpass the level of the average student taking the test, a youngster who does have a reading problem may do poorly on these tests. Not only might a child who has difficulty reading have trouble in comprehending the questions and the answers from among which the correct answer must be selected, but the child may also have insufficient time in which to complete the test. These tests are usually timed, and someone who must put extra time and effort into just reading the items may not have enough time to finish within the allotted time, much less have the time to go over the work and/or go back to items that were confusing.

Individually Administered Tests of Scholastic Aptitude

In contrast to group tests, individually administered scholastic aptitude tests are given to one child at a time. Since each child must be individually assessed with these tests, and a qualified psychologist must usually administer the test, it is much more costly, both of time and money, to administer individual tests. Thus, most school districts do not administer these tests on a regular basis to all students.

These tests are usually reserved for special instances. An individual test may be administered if the scores of a group test seem to be at odds with a child's classroom performance, if a child is being considered for a special program, or if a problem is suspected. The individual tests tend to be more reliable than the group tests and give more clues as to why a child may have performed poorly in a particular area. Although these tests are standardized tests in which there is a standard way to ask the questions and record the answers, the psychologist has the opportunity to see how the child acts during the test, to get an idea of why the child arrived at a particular answer, and to question the child as to why items were responded to as they were. Furthermore, in an individual test, the psychologist often reads each item to the child so that reading ability is not a factor in the ability to comprehend and respond to the items.

Among the more commonly individually administered tests are the *Wechsler Intelligence Scale for Children (WISC-III)* and the *Wechsler Preschool and Primary Scale of Intelligence (WPPSI-R)*, the *Stanford-Binet Intelligence Scale*, the *Detroit Tests of Learning Aptitude*, the *Kaufman Assessment Battery for Children (K-ABC)*, and the *Peabody Picture Vocabulary Test (PPVT-R)*. Most popular among these are the *WISC-III* and the *Stanford-Binet Intelligence Scale*, both of which have to be given by someone with specific training in administering the test. Most of these tests assess such abilities as verbal, quantitative, and abstract or spatial reasoning and short-term memory and include performance items as well as those requiring a verbal response. Many of these tests also test general knowledge that examinees of a particular age would be expected to know.

The *WISC-III*, for example, has a verbal scale that includes items on general information, similarities (how two things are alike), arithmetic reasoning, vocabulary, comprehension, and digit span (repetition of a span of numbers) and a performance scale that includes items requiring students to say what is missing in a picture, to put various pictures in order to tell a story, to replicate designs with blocks, to assemble items from their parts, to decipher codes, and to complete mazes.

The *Stanford-Binet Intelligence Scale* has sections on verbal reasoning, quantitative reasoning, abstract/visual reasoning, and short-term memory. The verbal reasoning section includes items on vocabulary, giving reasons for events, indicating what is wrong with various pictures, and identifying how things are alike or different; the quantitative reasoning section includes items on basic arithmetic computation and problem-solving skills, completing numerical sequences, and arranging the elements of an equation; the abstract/visual reasoning section requires the reproduction of patterns and designs, completing matrices, and identifying what folded and cut papers would look like when unfolded; and the short-term memory section requires repetition of sentences and numbers as well as identification of bead patterns and proper picture sequences.

Some simulated items typical of those on the *Wechsler Intelligence Scale for Children* are provided in Figure 5.4. The General Information, General Comprehension, and Arithmetic items are self-explanatory. On Picture Completion items, such as that shown in Figure 5.4, the child is requested to show what is missing from the picture; on Picture Arrangement items, the child is requested to sequence the three pictures so that they tell a story.

As you can see, the items differ from those found on achievement tests. Although some of the General Information and Arithmetic items may draw on information and skills learned in school, scholastic aptitude test items tend to be more general and tap a wider range of abilities than those that are directly taught in school. As previously mentioned, they are not designed to assess what has already been learned but to assess the skills related to future learning. That is, they are designed to predict school performance.

Most of the above-mentioned tests are highly verbal, however, and are not appropriate for students who have difficulty with the language. In addition to these tests there are a number of others that have been developed for use with children who either come from a non-English speaking background or who have language problems.

Culture-Fair and Language-Free Tests

Reading or language ability, particularly on the group tests, can seriously affect a child's performance on many of the scholastic aptitude tests. Cultural differences may also affect performance. For these reasons, attempts have been made to construct tests that are both language-free and culture-fair. Popular among these tests are the *Matrix Analogies Test*, the *Test of Nonverbal Intelligence (TONI-2)*, the *Leiter International Performance Scale*, the *Porteus Mazes*, and *Raven's Progressive Matrices*.

Typical of the items on these tests is the sample item from the *Matrix Analogies Test* illustrated in Figure 5.5. On this test, for example, the child is instructed to draw a circle around the picture that goes on the question mark. Although the instructions are verbal, they are brief and, once the child understands the task, the child can complete the rest of the test without further use of language.

Although these nonverbal tests provide a means of getting beyond the testing limitations imposed by language barriers, it is important to note that these tests have less predictive validity than do the individual and group aptitude tests described above. Success in school is, after all, related to one's

Figure 5.4
Simulated Items from the *Wechsler Intelligence Scale for Children*

General Information
1. How many wings does a bird have?
2. How many nickels make a dime?
3. What is steam made of?
4. Who wrote "Tom Sawyer?"
5. What is pepper?

General Comprehension
1. What should you do if you see someone forget his book when he leaves a restaurant?
2. What is the advantage of keeping money in a bank?
3. Why is copper often used in electric wires?

Arithmetic
1. Sam had three pieces of candy and Joe gave him four more. How many pieces of candy did Sam have altogether?
2. Three women divided eighteen golf balls equally among themselves. How many golf balls did each person receive?
3. If two buttons cost 15¢, what will be the cost of a dozen buttons?

Picture Completion

Picture Arrangement

Simulated items typical of those on the *Wechsler Intelligence Scale for Children* provided with permission for reproduction by The Psychological Corporation.

Figure 5.5
Sample Item from the *Matrix Analogies Test–Short Form*

From the *Matrix Analogies Test–Short Form.* Copyright © 1985 by the Psychological
  Corporation. Reproduced by permission. All rights reserved.

adaptation to the culture and one's ability to handle the language; youngsters
who have difficulty in these areas tend to have difficulty in school. Thus,
although culture-fair and language-free tests may provide an idea of a
child's problem-solving or reasoning ability in tasks that do not involve the
language or culture of the country, these tests are not as predictive of school
achievement as are other scholastic aptitude tests.

Many of the aptitude tests in current use have been criticized as being
biased or unfair to disadvantaged children or those from different cultures
because these children tend to do more poorly on these tests. Because
important decisions affecting children's lives are often made on the basis
of the scores on these tests, bias is an important issue. To establish that these
tests are biased as scholastic aptitude tests, however, one must be able to
show that the lowered performance on these tests is not related to lowered
performance in school. These tests may be biased as intelligence tests and
may not be assessing the ability of some children as well as that of others.
If children who do poorly on the test also do poorly in school, however, the

test is providing an accurate prediction of school performance. Disadvantaged students may do poorly on the test because they have not had the opportunities to acquire the skills that lead to school success. The problem may be a consequence of bias in our society and the lack of equal opportunities for all children, but the test is not biased for revealing this deficiency. The solution, therefore, is not to discard these tests but to put more time and energy into ensuring that all children have better access to the skills that are needed. At the same time, however, we must be sure that the tests are not misused. We must remember that they are not necessarily measures of intelligence, that the scores are subject to change, and that their predictive ability is far from perfect.

One approach to this problem has been the development of the System of Multicultural Pluralistic Assessment (SOMPA), which is an approach to testing designed to take language and cultural differences into account in estimating a child's cognitive, perceptual, and psychomotor abilities. It consists of both a parent interview and a student assessment. At the parent interview, which may be conducted in English or Spanish, a sociocultural and a health history scale are given as well as the *Adaptive Behavior Inventory for Children*, which asks the parents questions regarding how the child manages in everyday situations. The student assessment includes various physical measures as well as the *Bender Visual Motor Gestalt* test and a scholastic aptitude test such as the *WISC-III*. Rather than examining the scores of the scholastic aptitude test in isolation, however, a system of interpretation is used that corrects the scores for cultural and linguistic differences. The adjusted scores assess the child's learning ability in a setting in which the cultural differences would not be a factor. It should be noted, however, that cultural differences often do impact on a child's success in school and, to the extent that language or cultural factors are interfering with the attainment of needed knowledge and skills, they cannot be ignored as a factor in predicting school performance.

College Entrance Examinations

One type of scholastic aptitude examination that most high school students and their parents are acutely aware of are the college entrance examinations. Prior to admission, most colleges request students to take either the *ACT Assessment*, administered by the American College Testing Program, or the *Scholastic Assessment Tests (SAT)*, administered by the College Entrance Examination Board. The *Scholastic Assessment Tests* include both the *SAT I: Reasoning Test*, previously known as the *Scholastic*

Aptitude Test (SAT), and the *SAT II: Subject Tests*, previously known as the *College Board Achievement Tests*. In this chapter, however, the focus will be on only the *SAT I: Reasoning Test* rather than on the *SAT II: Subject Tests*.

The SAT I: Reasoning Test

This test is designed to assess the underlying abilities needed to perform well in college rather than the mastery of the content in a particular course. The *SAT I: Reasoning Test* is divided into sections on verbal and numerical reasoning. In the past, the verbal sections of the *Scholastic Aptitude Test* have included four types of multiple choice questions: antonyms, analogies, sentence completions, and reading comprehension. Although the *SAT I: Reasoning Test* is similar, the antonym questions have been eliminated and greater emphasis has been placed on the reading passages; the reading passages are longer and a greater proportion of the questions are on these passages. The mathematical section includes items on arithmetic, geometry, and algebra but, in contrast to the *Scholastic Aptitude Test*, on which all the items were in the multiple choice format, the *SAT I: Reasoning Test* includes items on which the students must produce their own answers rather than select the answer from the choices provided. Additionally, students are encouraged to use calculators when taking the mathematical sections of the test. It is assumed that students taking the test have had at least a year of algebra and some geometry. Although students who take more advanced courses in mathematics tend to do better on the test because of their greater facility in mathematical reasoning, the test does not assess knowledge of more advanced mathematics. The questions are primarily on arithmetic, algebra, and geometry, including some on statistics, probability, and data interpretation. There is increased emphasis on mathematical reasoning and applications to real life settings. Sample items are included in Figure 5.6.

You may note that although some of the numerical items are similar to those that might be found on classroom tests, the items require students to make connections and see relationships that go beyond the content taught in a specific course. These items are assessing a student's ability to reason about the concepts and apply them to new situations. In the verbal items, also, what is being assessed is not the ability to define vocabulary words or to state grammatical rules but to apply this knowledge in novel situations.

It should be noted that although most of the sample items are multiple choice and the *Scholastic Aptitude Test* was a multiple-choice examination, the *SAT I: Reasoning Test* does include new formats that require students to formulate their own answers to questions rather than simply select the correct answer from the ones provided. The mathematics item in Figure 5.6

that requires a student-produced response is an example of the new item-types that are included. Although the form of the items has changed, however, the test still assesses critical thinking and reasoning skills as opposed to subject-area content.

Although the scores are not submitted to the colleges, many students also take the *Preliminary Scholastic Aptitude Test (PSAT)*. This test is a short version of the *SAT* that students usually take as high school juniors. It is used to give students an idea of how they are likely to perform on the *SAT*—adding a zero to the *PSAT* score gives the predicted *SAT* score. The *PSAT* is also used as the qualifying examination for the National Merit Scholarships.

The ACT Assessment

In contrast to the *SAT*, the *ACT Assessment* includes tests in four areas: English, mathematics, reading, and science reasoning. Although these tests are more content-oriented than the *SAT I: Reasoning Test*, they also focus on the application of reasoning and problem-solving skills to material drawn from these areas as opposed to the recall of the factual material that might have been taught in a particular course. All of the items included in the *ACT Assessment* are multiple choice in format; sample items from these tests are included in Figure 5.7.

The English Test measures understanding of the conventions of standard written English as well as rhetorical skills. In addition to a total score on the English Test, students also receive a Usage/Mechanics subscore, which reflects performance on the punctuation, grammar, and sentence structure items, and a Rhetorical Skills subscore, which reflects performance on the items covering strategy, organization, and style of written presentation. The sample English Test items in Figure 5.7 are representative of the items contributing to the Usage/Mechanics subscore although not all items on the English Test are in this format. In the sample provided, each item refers to the underlined section of the accompanying passage that is similarly numbered. If the underlined section is correct, the NO CHANGE option is the correct response; if the underlined section is not correct, the correct response is the option that would be correct in that context. Although students may study grammar, punctuation, and sentence structure in particular classes, the items are not testing the ability to recall verbatim rules or parts of speech; they are testing language usage skills.

The Mathematics Test requires the use of reasoning skills to solve practical problems in mathematics such as those in Figure 5.7. Although the mathematics items are based on information learned in school, the emphasis

Figure 5.6
Sample Items from the *SAT I: Reasoning Test*

Sentence Completion
(Examinees must select the pair of words that best fits the meaning of the sentence.)

Like a parasite organism, the most detested
character in the play depended on others
for ---- and ---- nothing.

(A)   ideas..required
(B)   diversion..spared
(C)   assistance..destroyed
(D)   survival..consumed
(E)   sustenance..returned

Analogies
(Examinees must select the pair of words that best represents the relationship in the capitalized pair.)

PACT:NATIONS::

(A)   compromise:extremes
(B)   certificate:qualifications
(C)   treaty:hostilities
(D)   border:municipalities
(E)   contract:parties

is on the application of basic mathematical knowledge and reasoning rather than extensive computation or the recall of complex formulae or rules. The content of the Mathematics Test is drawn from pre-algebra, elementary algebra, intermediate algebra and coordinate geometry, plane geometry, and trigonometry. All of the items are multiple choice and, in addition to a total score on the Mathematics Test, three subscores are also reported: a subscore in Pre-Algebra/Elementary Algebra, a subscore in Intermediate Algebra/Coordinate Geometry, and a subscore in Plane Geometry/Trigonometry.

As you may note in Figure 5.7, reading comprehension skills are obviously required in order to do well on the Science Reasoning Test. The Science Reasoning Test, however, emphasizes the interpretation, evaluation, reasoning, and problem-solving skills required in the natural sciences rather than reading ability. The content of the items is drawn from biology, chemistry, physics, and earth/space sciences, and some background knowledge in science is assumed. Advanced knowledge of these subjects is not required; the test is designed to assess science reasoning skills rather than the recall of specific scientific content. Referring, for example, to the Science Reasoning Test items in Figure 5.7, you can see that all the specific

Figure 5.6 (continued)

Mathematics: Multiple-choice

When three times a number n is added to 7, the result is 22.

Which of the following statements represents the statement above?

(A) $3 + n + 7 = 22$
(B) $n + (3 \times 7) = 22$
(C) $3(n + 7) = 22$
(D) $3 + 7n = 22$
(E) $3n + 7 = 22$

Mathematics: Student-produced Response

The entire surface of a solid cube with edge of length 6 inches is painted. The cube is then cut into cubes each with edge of length 1 inch. How many of the smaller cubes have paint on exactly 1 face?

Quantitative Comparisons

(Examinees must answer A, if the quantity on the left is greater
B, if the quantity on the right is greater
C, if the two quantities are equal
D, if the relationship can't be determined from the information given.)

n percent of 50 is greater than 40.

n	90

SAT questions selected from *Taking the SAT I Reasoning Test (March, May, & June 1994)*, College Entrance Examination Board, 1993. Reprinted by permission of Educational Testing Service, the copyright owner of the test questions. Permission to reprint the above material does not constitute review or endorsement by Educational Testing Service or the College Board of this publication as a whole or of any other questions or testing information it may contain.

knowledge needed to answer the questions is provided in the passage. The items are not testing the students' knowledge of dinosaurs, but the students' ability to interpret, evaluate, and draw conclusions from the scientific information provided in the passage.

In contrast to the Science Reasoning Test, the content of the items on the Reading Test is not drawn from the writing in any particular subject area; passages are selected from prose fiction or topics in social studies, the

Figure 5.7
Sample Items from the *ACT Assessment*

Mathematics Test

Which of the following expresses 60 as a product of prime numbers?

(A) 2x3x5
(B) 2x2x15
(C) 2x2x3x5
(D) 1x2x5x6

If the area of a triangle is 18 square units and its base is 3 units long, how many units long is the altitude to that base?

(A) 3
(B) 6
(C) 12
(D) 15
(E) 33

English Test

(Each item refers to the similarly numbered underlined section of the passage. Students must indicate whether the section is best as written or whether it would be better to change it as indicated in one of the options.)

What teases us with the giddy possibilities of freedom better than a videocassette recorder? There are few things that seem to promise so much for so little effort. Program the right channel, set the timer, and even the late-late-late movie is within grasp. Neither storm nor sleep will keep a
₁₆
well-running VCR from its appointed task.

In fact, a VCR can free us from the tyranny of the television schedule altogether. With video stores almost as prevalent as fast-food restaurants. The desire
₁₇
to finally see the conclusion of a movie can be as readily satisfied as the urge for a burger and fries.
₁₈

[1] Unfortunately, the *us* I've been talking about doesn't including me. [2] For example, I have several
₁₉
versions of Alfred Hitchcock's mystery-comedy *The 39 Steps* none of them includes the last fifteen minutes.
₂₀

16. **F.** NO CHANGE
    G. Neither, storm nor
    H. Neither storm nor,
    J. Neither storm, nor

17. **A.** NO CHANGE
    B. restaurants, the
    C. restaurants; the
    D. restaurants, and the

18. **F.** NO CHANGE
    G. the urge by one
    H. you can satisfy the urge
    J. the urge can be satisfied by one

19. **A.** NO CHANGE
    B. doesn't include I.
    C. didn't include me.
    D. doesn't include me.

20. **F.** NO CHANGE
    G. *Steps,* but
    H. *Steps* which
    J. *Steps,* where

Figure 5.7 (continued)

Science Reasoning Test

Two paleontologists discuss their theories about various characteristics of dinosaurs.

Paleontologist 1

Dinosaurs were large endothermic (warm-blooded) creatures that were physiologically more advanced than the ectothermic (cold-blooded) reptiles. Rather than depending on sunlight or ambient air temperature to warm themselves, as would reptiles, dinosaurs were able to metabolically regulate their body temperatures. Endothermy allowed them to survive in temperatures that would have been lethal to most ectotherms.

Evidence for endothermy includes the discovery of many dinosaur bones in regions of Earth that were arctic during the dinosaur's time. Had the dinosaurs been ectotherms, they would have been forced to constantly sun themselves in order to maintain a stable, warm body temperature. Because this would have been impossible during the dark arctic winter, it seems likely that the dinosaurs were endotherms. Like birds (also endotherms), certain dinosaurs evolved featherlike structures that may have served to insulate them from cold temperatures.

The ratio of predators to prey in some dinosaur communities matches that of fossil mammal communities (low number of predators to high number of prey), indicating that the dinosaurs may have had dietary requirements similar to those of the mammals. Additionally, the bone structure of dinosaurs, with its many blood vessels (highly vascularized), seems virtually identical to that of mammals.

Paleontologist 2

Dinosaurs were large ectothermic reptiles that relied on their enormous mass to act as a heat reservoir and stabilize their body temperature. This forced dinosaurs living in seasonally cold regions to migrate to warmer, sunnier regions for the winter. Likewise, the featherlike structures found on some dinosaurs may have helped shield them from the intense summer sun.

Recent investigations of modern ectothermic communities reveal predator-prey ratios similar to those observed in endotherm communities. In addition, although dinosaur bones exhibit a high degree of vascularization (similar to that of mammals), such a pattern has been observed in the bones of numerous modern reptiles. Also, many small birds and mammals have been found to produce bones that are low in vascularization.

29. If the theory of Paleontologist 1 is correct, and dinosaurs were alive in Earth's present climate, what geographical distribution on land could be expected for them?

   A. They could live only in arctic and antarctic regions.
   B. They could live only in temperate to tropical regions.
   C. They could live almost anywhere on Earth.
   D. They could not survive anywhere on Earth.

30. Which of the following would most effectively support the theory of Paleontologist 2 ?

   F. Large, modern reptiles that live year-round in northern Alaska
   G. Large, modern reptiles that exhibit seasonal migration
   H. Modern endotherms that are capable of lowering their body temperature during periods of hibernation
   J. Modern endotherms that have evolved insulating structures

31. When one observes low numbers of predators and high numbers of their prey in a stable community, it can be inferred that the predators are endotherms because endotherms:

   A. require more energy to maintain their constant body temperature than do ectotherms of the same size.
   B. look for prey only at night when the temperature is lower.
   C. store energy as fat for use during hibernation.
   D. must run faster than ectotherms to catch their prey.

32. An important concept that underlies both paleontologists' hypotheses is that:

   F. endotherms always have a higher body temperature than ectotherms.
   G. tropical plants can be artificially grown in cold climates.
   H. some characteristics of extinct animals can be determined from their fossil remains.
   J. the fossil bone shapes of dinosaurs were similar to those of modern reptiles.

33. Assuming that dinosaurs were ectotherms, which of the following adaptations might have allowed them to maintain a near-constant body temperature?

   A. Regulating their body temperatures by moving back and forth between sunny areas and shady areas
   B. Decreasing blood circulation through their bones
   C. Having bones that grow only part of the year
   D. Increasing blood circulation through their bones

34. Which of the following characteristics is most inconsistent with the theory that dinosaurs were endotherms?

   F. Large numbers of blood vessels in dinosaur bones
   G. Their ability to live in cold regions
   H. The presence of featherlike structures on some dinosaurs
   J. Their reptilian appearance

humanities, or natural sciences and, in addition to a total Reading Test score, separate subscores are provided in Social Studies/Sciences and Arts/Literature reading skills. The test assesses the ability to derive implicit meaning from a written passage as well as to make comparisons, generalize, and draw conclusions on the basis of what was read.

Interpreting SAT and ACT Scores

The scores on the *SAT* and *ACT* are reported on different scales: the *SAT* verbal and numerical scores are reported on a scale of 200 to 800 while the total scores on the *ACT* Reading Test, Science Test, Science Reasoning Test, Mathematics Test, and English Test are reported on a scale of 1 to 36. Furthermore, subscores are reported on the *ACT* reading, mathematics, and English tests. These subscores are reported on a scale of 1 to 18. In addition to the scale scores on the *SAT* and *ACT*, the score report for each of the tests will indicate the percentile rank of each score; that is, the percentage of students in different categories who fell at or below the score obtained. The meaning of these scores is explained more fully in Chapter 9.

Because college-bound students and their parents view these tests as so important, there has been considerable interest in coaching courses that claim to help students increase their scores, particularly on the *SAT I*. Although many of the companies offering these courses claim to be able to significantly raise a student's score, the results of independent research on the effects of coaching indicate that much more modest gains are achieved than are often advertised. A recent summary of the research on coaching by Donald E. Powers (1993) indicates, on average, a small effect on the old verbal *Scholastic Aptitude Test* scores of between 1 and 3 points with a somewhat larger effect, of about 17 points, on the numerical scores. This gain is the effect attributed to coaching over and above that which could be attributed to other causes.

Many students will do better on a second testing regardless of whether or not they have taken a coaching course and some students have shown gains as high as 100 points on the *SAT*. Practice and familiarity with the test format as well as the effect of growth, however, may account for the gain. Furthermore, many students—even those who have had coaching courses— have lower scores on a second testing, although the companies that offer these courses rarely mention those students in their advertising.

Although both the *SAT* and the *ACT Assessment* are relatively reliable, they are not perfect. Although measurement error may result in some students scoring lower than would be expected on a first testing, others may score higher than expected and then do worse on a second testing. In general, students who score unusually low show the largest gains on a second testing, while those who score unusually high show the smallest gains and are even likely to score lower on a second testing. If a youngster has performed better than expected on a first testing, the likelihood of improvement on a second testing—even with coaching—is less than if the performance had been lower than expected. Coaching is more likely to help a student who has done more poorly than expected. Even if the student might be able to raise the score without coaching, the coaching may impose a discipline and focus on the requirements of the test that might not otherwise occur. Coaching is a family decision; it can't hurt but it is important to remember that although some students certainly do show significant gains after taking a coaching course, many do not. Although large gains are more likely for students with lower scores and those who do more poorly than expected, there is no absolute way to determine who will gain, whether the gain would have occurred even in the absence of the course, or even if the scores will go down.

When taking these tests, remember that colleges do not make admissions decisions on one score alone. Considerable weight is also put on a student's high-school grades, the nature of the courses that a student took, and other information—such as extracurricular activities, jobs, and volunteer work—that indicates a student's ability to do well at the institution. In fact, there are a number of institutions, including some of the elite liberal arts colleges, that do not require students to submit such scores.

Although, in general, students with high aptitude test scores tend to do well in college, the validity of these scores is far from perfect. There are many good colleges that accept students with relatively low scores, and low scores no more mean that a student will necessarily do poorly in college than high scores guarantee success. Most colleges accept those students they believe will be successful, and students from the same high school with very different scores may do equally well at the different colleges they attend.

VOCATIONAL APTITUDE TESTS

In addition to scholastic aptitude tests, many schools also administer vocational aptitude tests to secondary school students. The purpose of these tests is to help identify occupational areas in which a child may be success-ful. These tests fall into two general categories: (1) those tests that assess a child's strengths and weaknesses, and (2) those that assess interests. The interest inventories are not aptitude tests in the same sense as the other tests discussed. Rather than tests in which there is one right answer to a question, these instruments are questionnaires on which there are no right answers. Instead, each different response indicates a different predisposition, and the pattern of an individual's responses provides a summary of that person's interests.

Differential Aptitude Testing

Those vocational aptitude tests that focus on a child's strengths and weaknesses are similar to the group-administered achievement and scholastic aptitude tests previously described. They differ somewhat, however, in that they tend to measure more than only school abilities. The *Differential Aptitude Tests*, for example, include subtests on spatial relations, mechanical reasoning, and clerical speed and accuracy, as well as on the more school-related areas of verbal reasoning, numerical ability, abstract reasoning, and language usage. Another frequently used vocational aptitude test is the *General Aptitude Test Battery*, which is published by the United States Employment Service. In addition to verbal aptitude, numerical ability, and arithmetic reasoning, this test also measures spatial aptitude, form perception, clerical perception, motor coordination, manual dexterity, and finger dexterity.

Figure 5.8 includes items from the *Differential Aptitude Tests* typical of those found on this type of test. As you may note, the items testing verbal and numerical aptitude are quite similar to those found on other scholastic aptitude tests. The items in the other areas, however, focus on skills not tested on the general scholastic aptitude tests and are more closely related to the skills required in the performance of specific jobs.

If we look at how well these tests predict future academic or job performance, we find that numerical and verbal tests are good predictors of success in all school subjects, even the more job-related subjects such as typing or industrial arts. There seems to be a general academic ability which underlies success in most school subjects and which is apparently measured by these tests. The important question, however, is whether these tests are also useful in helping a child to determine the areas in which she or he is likely to be successful in the future. Or, to put it another way, do people with high scores in manual and finger dexterity, for example, do well as dentists and/or electronic assemblers?

The manual for the *General Aptitude Test Battery* does indicate relatively high validity coefficients between some of the subtests and various occupations. The subtests having the highest validity coefficients for predicting

Figure 5.8
Sample Items from the *Differential Aptitude Tests: 5th Edition, Form C*

Verbal Reasoning

This is a test to see how well you can reason with words. Each sentence has two words missing — the first word and the last word. Each answer choice has a pair of words that is related to the words in the sentence in some way. The first word of the pair should fit at the beginning of the sentence so that the first two words in the sentence are related to each other in a certain way. The second word of the pair should fit at the end of the sentence so that the second two words in the sentence are related to each other in the same way as the first two words. When you have chosen the pair that you feel *best* completes the sentence, mark the letter of that pair on your answer document.

> ...... is to right as west is to ......
>
> F   left —— north
> G   direction —— east
> H   left —— south
> J   wrong —— direction
> K   left —— east

Numerical Reasoning

> What number should replace P in this correct addition example?
>
> $$\begin{array}{r} 5P \\ +\ 2 \\ \hline 58 \end{array}$$
>
> F   3
> G   4
> H   7
> J   9
> K   None of these

Abstract Reasoning

This is a test to see how well you can reason with figures or designs. Each problem has four Problem Figures and five Answer Figures. The four Problem Figures form a series with something happening in each Problem Figure. You are to choose the Answer Figure that should be the next figure (or the fifth one) in the series. Then mark the space on your answer document for the answer you have chosen.

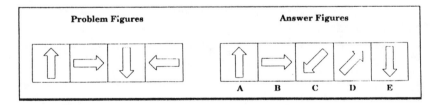

Figure 5.8 (continued)

Perceptual Speed and Accuracy

This is a test to see how quickly and correctly you can compare letter/number combinations. Each problem contains five letter/number combinations. These five combinations also appear after the problem number on your answer sheet, but the combinations are in a different order. For each problem in your test booklet, one of the five combinations is *underlined*. You are to look at the underlined combination and find the same one on your answer sheet. Then fill in the circle under it.

A	AB	AC	AD	AE	AF
B	aA	aB	BA	Ba	Bb
C	A7	7A	B7	7B	AB
D	Aa	Ba	bA	BA	bB
E	3A	3B	33	B3	BB

Mechanical Reasoning

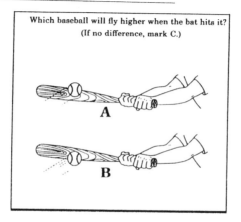

Which baseball will fly higher when the bat hits it?
(If no difference, mark C.)

A

B

Space Relations

This test consists of patterns with shading or designs on them. These patterns can be folded to make three-dimensional shapes. Each problem shows one pattern, followed by four three-dimensional figures. You are to choose the one figure that can be made from the pattern. Then mark the space on your answer document for the answer you have chosen.

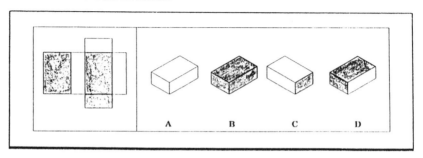

A B C D

success as an electronic assembler, for example, are finger dexterity and manual dexterity, and the tests with the highest validity coefficients for predicting success as a stenographer-typist are numerical and clerical perception.

Even these coefficients tend to be relatively low, however, and if a child gets a high score on a subtest that is predictive of success in one area, this score does not mean that he or she wouldn't be equally or more successful in a completely different field. While it is interesting to note that the highest score of general office clerks on the *General Aptitude Test Battery* is on the Clerical Perception test, for example, computer programmers, whose highest score is on the General Intelligence test, score even higher on clerical perception than do the general office clerks.

These tests are used by school counselors to help a child in defining his or her interests and in exploring possible careers. It must be noted, however, that the results of these tests are in no way definitive. They are best used as a basis for discussion and further exploration, not as final decision-making tools. There is a question about the differential validity of the various scales and, regardless of how well a student may perform on a particular test, the youngster may not be happy in a vocational area requiring that skill if his or her interests do not lie in that direction.

Often, therefore, secondary schools administer vocational interest inventories in addition to (or in lieu of) the more traditional aptitude tests. Although not usually categorized as aptitude tests, these interest inventories are used as predictors of vocational satisfaction in different areas of work. In some cases, test publishers package a vocational aptitude test with an interest inventory as a career exploration tool. The *Career Interest Inventory*, for example, was standardized with the *Differential Aptitude Tests*, and administration of the two instruments together enables the counselor to examine a youngster's aptitude scores in relation to the child's interests. Similarly, the *Occupational Aptitude Survey and Interest Schedule (OASIS-2)* also consists of two tests normed on the same sample of students, the *OASIS-2 Aptitude Survey* and the *OASIS-2 Interest Schedule*.

Vocational Interest Inventories

Vocational interest inventories are used to explore a student's interests in relationship to different jobs or professions. Most well known among these are the *Strong Interest Inventory*, the *Kuder Occupational Interest Survey* and, for use with somewhat younger children, the *Kuder General*

Interest Survey. Other such instruments currently used in the schools are the *OASIS-2 Interest Schedule* referred to above, the *Career Interest Inventory*, the *Ohio Vocational Interest Survey*, the *Gordon Occupational Check List*, the *Campbell Interest and Skill Survey*, and the *Career Assessment Inventory*. The difference among these instruments is primarily in the form of the items and the occupations or activities to which students are expected to respond. On the *Gordon Occupational Check List*, for example, students rate a number of activities related to occupations not requiring a college degree, while the *Campbell Interest and Skill Survey* focuses on careers that require a post-secondary education.

The *Strong Interest Inventory* and the *Kuder Occupational Interest Survey* represent different approaches to the assessment of an individual's interests. On the *Strong Interest Inventory*, students must indicate whether they like, dislike, or are indifferent to various occupations, activities, and types of people. In addition, there is also a section of the inventory in which students choose which of two activities they prefer and one in which they assess their own personal characteristics. On the *Kuder Occupational Interest Inventory*, different types of activities are grouped together and, within each grouping, students must indicate which activities they most and least enjoy. This type of scale is called a forced-choice format because, unlike the *Strong Interest Inventory*, on which students can say they are indifferent to just about every item, students taking the *Kuder Occupational Interest Survey* must choose which activity they like the most and which they like the least.

Items typical of those on these two types of instruments are illustrated in Figure 5.9. For each group of three items on the *Kuder Occupational Interest Survey*, the student must indicate which activity they like the most (M) and which they like the least (L); they are forced to make a choice. The items on the *Strong*, however, do not force students to make comparisons among different activities. Students may indicate indifference to an occupation, may say that they can't decide which activity they prefer, or which characteristics describe them. They are not required to indicate what they prefer the most or the least. It is possible for them to say that they like everything, dislike everything, or are indifferent to everything. They can give the same response to every item. In technical terms, the tendency to respond to every item in a similar fashion is referred to as a response set. The tendency to say they like everything is sometimes called acquiescence or yea-saying, while the tendency to say they dislike everything may be referred to as nay-saying. Other response sets include the tendency to select neutral responses or to respond in a socially desirable way, that is, to select

Figure 5.9
Sample Items from the *Strong Interest Inventory* and *Kuder Occupational Interest Survey*

Sample Items from the Revised Strong Interest Inventory

2	L	I	D*	Actor/Actress
14	L	I	D	Auto mechanic
21	L	I	D	Bilingual teacher
38	L	I	D	Criminal lawyer
39	L	I	D	Computer programmer
86	L	I	D	Nurse
132	L	I	D	Word processor
178	L	I	D	Cooking
180	L	I	D	Writing reports
203	L	I	D	Looking at things in a clothing store
218	L	I	D	Climbing along the edge of a steep cliff
230	L	I	D	Playing team sports with friends

PART VI. PREFERENCE BETWEEN TWO ACTIVITIES

275	Dealing with things	L = R**	Dealing with people
279	Outside work	L = R	Inside work
283	Being friends with a research scientist	L = R	Being friends with a sales executive
296	Reading a book	L = R	Watching TV or going to a movie

PART VII. YOUR CHARACTERISTICS

300	Y	?	N***	Usually start activities of my group
301	Y	?	N	Prefer working alone rather than on committees
307	Y	?	N	Can communicate easily with people of different cultures
311	Y	?	N	Have patience when teaching others

* L = Like, I = Indifferent, D = Dislike
** L = Prefer item on left, R = prefer item on right, = means like or dislike both items the same or can't decide.
*** Y = Yes, N = No, ? = can't decide.

Sample Items from the *Kuder Occupational Interest Survey*

Visit an art gallery	M	L
Browse in a library	M	L
Visit a museum	M	L
Collect autographs	M	L
Collect coins	M	L
Collect stones	M	L

Reproduced from *Kuder Occupational Interest Survey* by permission of the publisher, CTB/McGraw-Hill. Copyright © 1985 by G. Frederic Kuder.

the response that is perceived to be most socially acceptable as opposed to the one that really describes the student's opinion.

Although students may occasionally try to "fake" their responses, most students understand that these inventories are designed to help them, and they do try to respond as honestly as possible. Many youngsters at this age do not have the insight to know what they really like or dislike, however, or even what is involved in the different careers or activities to which they are responding. In the face of this uncertainty, students may exhibit a response set even though they have consciously decided to do so. The forced-choice format was designed to overcome this tendency but it also poses problems; on instruments such as the *Kuder Occupational Interest Inventory*, students are forced to choose one activity as most desirable even when they truly find two or three choices to be equally appealing.

On many of these interest inventories, the interpretation of the score is based on how a student's responses compare to those of individuals who are successful and/or satisfied in different vocational/professional areas. The question to be answered is whether the youngster's profile is closer to the profile of lawyers, for example, than it is to that of engineers or doctors. Comparing a student's profile with that of successful employees in a field, however, may be misleading. Even if there were no problem with defining success and/or satisfaction, one doesn't know what current employees' interests were like when those employees were still high school students. Their current interests may have developed as a consequence of their career choice and not the reverse. We don't know, for example, whether the score profile that a successful lawyer has today is the same as that same lawyer would have had if he or she had been tested in high school. It may be that a lawyer's abilities are shaped by experiences in law school and on the job and that, had today's successful lawyers been tested while still in high school, their responses would have been different.

Some interest inventories provide the names of specific occupations that are compatible with a student's interests; some provide general interest areas such as scientific, artistic, persuasive, social service, or mechanical; and others provide some combination of the two. Several of these instruments also categorize individuals into different vocational personality types based on a set of six general occupational themes developed by John L. Holland (1985): realistic, investigative, artistic, social, enterprising, and conventional. Each of these occupational themes is then linked with a number of different occupations that supposedly involve activities compatible with that theme.

Regardless of the type of information provided, however, the scores that a youngster receives on a vocational interest inventory should not be taken as a definitive indicator of the areas in which the child will find satisfaction or be successful. Not only are there the problems described above with the different types of scales, but adolescence is a volatile time in a young person's life, and interests expressed at that time are often unstable. Indeed, many youngsters have been exposed to only a limited number of possible options and haven't even thought about many areas in which they may later develop an interest. Rather, these tests are best used as a basis for discussion and exploration of possible interests and avenues for further exploration.

Vocational aptitude tests and interest inventories share with other aptitude tests the intent of predicting future performance. It must be reiterated, however, that the scores on none of these instruments may be taken as definitive. Even where the predictive validity of an aptitude test is high—and those of the scholastic aptitude tests tend to be higher than those of the vocational aptitude tests—we never know how predictive the scores will be for a particular individual. High predictive validity indicates that, *in general*, individuals who score well on the test will do well in the area in which performance is being predicted. A test that is highly predictive for one individual—or even for most individuals—may not be valid for a particular child. Scores on aptitude tests can provide helpful information for future planning but should always supplement rather than supplant other available information.

REFERENCES

Powers, Donald E. (Summer, 1993). Coaching for the SAT: A summary of the summaries and an update. *Educational Measurement: Issues and Practice, 12*(2), 24–30.

Holland, John L. (1985). *Making vocational choices: A theory of vocational personalities and work environments* (2d ed.). Englewood Cliffs, N.J.: Prentice Hall.

Chapter 6

Assessing Personality and Attitudes

Imagine a suburban classroom in which Jennifer, a fifth-grader, is causing concern. She is reluctant to participate in classroom activities, is often disruptive and antagonistic toward other children, and frequently seems to be daydreaming rather than attending to her classwork. She frequently complains of being picked on by the other children and makes excessive demands for attention from her teacher. While her performance on standardized achievement and aptitude tests is above average, her classroom performance is weak. She rarely completes assignments, and the work that she does is messy and full of careless errors. Understandably, both her teacher and her parents are concerned about her behavior.

It is in situations such as this that personality testing may be done. Most schools do not administer personality tests as a matter of course but reserve them for situations in which a problem is suspected. Not only must many of these tests be individually administered and/or interpreted by a psychologist, which is quite time consuming, but since these tests probe issues of a personal nature, there is also the concern that they may be construed as an invasion of privacy. It is therefore unlikely for a school to administer personality tests without prior discussion with the child's parents or guardian and without their consent.

PERSONALITY TESTING

Personality tests focus on the traits or dispositions that are assumed to affect the way individuals respond to their environment. It should be noted, however, that there is no general agreement on either the traits that define an individual's personality or even the existence of an enduring set of personality characteristics. Thus, there are a wide variety of approaches to personality assessment.

Some personality tests attempt to describe the individual's underlying dispositions—traits such as aggression or sociability that are assumed to be relatively stable and enduring characteristics of the individual. Others focus on identifying the problems that are facing an individual at a particular time. While some of these tests attempt to identify individuals with pathology, others simply describe the characteristics of normal people. Regardless of the approach, however, the purpose of these tests is to help explain why people act the way they do rather than to rate their performance.

When we speak of personality tests, we are not referring to tests in the usual sense. There is no one correct answer to the items on these instruments, and there may not even be a single score but a pattern of scores that yields a particular diagnosis or description of the individual. These tests take many forms: in some instances the individual—or even a child's teacher or parents—may respond to a series of questions; in other cases a psychologist may ask a child to describe an inkblot or make up a story about a picture. Regardless of the form, however, personality assessment tends to be less valid and reliable than the assessment of achievement or aptitude, and much greater caution should be used in interpreting the scores. With that caveat, let's examine some different approaches to personality assessment.

Informal Assessment of Personality

Much of the personality assessment that occurs in school is informal and initiated by the classroom teacher. Typical of these informal methods of assessment are the anecdotal records of classroom behavior that teachers keep and the sociometric or "guess who" techniques that are used to get a sense of the social interaction among the children in a class.

Anecdotal Records

Anecdotal records, in which a teacher keeps informal, descriptive records of a child's behavior in class, are one way of recording how a student behaves in a natural setting. One of the problems with anecdotal records, however, is that teachers have many responsibilities in the classroom and are limited in the amount of time that they can spend recording behavior. Although unusual events may draw their attention, they cannot possibly observe the behavior of all of the children all of the time. Furthermore, the events that draw a teacher's attention are often determined by the teacher's own biases and expectations, as well as by the degree to which a child's behavior disrupts other classroom activities. A quiet act of kindness by an otherwise rambunctious child is less likely to be noticed than one more episode of mischief. Children who act out in class tend to be much more noticeable than those who may be facing equally serious emotional problems but whose behavior is more reserved. Anecdotal records are also subject to incomplete and distorted recollections, particularly if there is a time lapse between the occurrence of the behavior and the time when it is recorded.

Anecdotal records are most useful when the teacher records the event soon after it occurs, when the anecdote includes a full description of the event rather than an inference or interpretation of what occurred, and when the record includes descriptions of a number of events occurring over a period of time. It is more helpful to indicate that Jonathan refused to shake Michael's hand after losing to him in a tennis match than to say that Jonathan was jealous of Michael's victory. Jealousy, or any other emotion, can only be inferred and may not be the reason for the behavior. It is only after a number of anecdotes are recorded that typical patterns of behavior become clear and hypotheses may be advanced as to their causes. Even then, causal hypotheses should be very tentative.

In describing the behavior of others, people tend to see actions that support their expectations and miss those that contradict them. Furthermore, there is what is referred to as a "halo" effect in making judgments about others. This effect occurs when one's overall impression of someone colors the assessment of particular events. Assume, for example, that Melissa has just given an oral book report in which she has mixed up the names of the characters. If Melissa is perceived as a well-behaved, conscientious student, the teacher may attribute this error to nervousness and ignore it. If, on the other hand, Melissa is viewed as uncooperative and careless in her work, this same behavior may be noted as one more example confirming her carelessness.

As you can see, then, this type of informal assessment is very subjective. Not only are particular events colored by the preconceptions of the raters but so is the judgment as to which events are significant. In contrast, the use of structured tests provides a standard set of behaviors that are consistently applied to all students being assessed. Additionally, norms are often available for published personality tests, enabling one to ascertain whether or not the responses of a particular child are within the normal range. The use of anecdotal records, however, can add to the information provided by a more structured personality test and may expand upon the information obtained from a more formal instrument.

Sociometric and "Guess Who" Techniques

Other types of informal personality assessments, such as sociometric or "guess who" techniques, are used in the classroom to help identify youngsters who may be socially isolated or rejected by other children in a class. Rather than relying on the assessment of the teacher, however, these techniques are based on students' responses toward other students in a class.

In doing a sociometric analysis, students are typically asked to list a specified number of other students in the class with whom they would or would not like to engage in various activities. They may be asked, for example, with whom they would like to work on various projects, with whom they would like to play, eat, or be seated, or whom they would like to invite to their home or to a birthday party. From the students' responses, a teacher can get a sense of the social groupings in a class, can see the reciprocity of choices, and can identify children who are rejected by the others. This technique is often used as an aid in making classroom groupings and can help a teacher in identifying a child who may need help.

A similar technique is the "guess who" technique in which students are asked to identify the students who fit a particular description. They may be asked to guess who is always smiling or who is always sad or to name the students who are popular or those who never want to participate in class. As with the sociometric technique, the "guess who" technique can help a teacher identify youngsters who are perceived in a negative way by others in the class as well as those who tend to be ignored.

The purpose of these informal techniques is not to describe a child's personality or identify specific personality problems. Instead, they may sensitize the teacher to the social climate in the classroom and help to identify youngsters with social or emotional difficulties. Children identified through these informal techniques may then be referred for more formal testing with a personality inventory or projective technique.

Self-Report Inventories versus Ratings by Others

A self-report inventory is a personality measure on which individuals respond to a series of questions about themselves. Among such instruments commonly used in the schools are the *Mooney Problem Check List*, the *Adjective Check List*, the *Minnesota Multiphasic Personality Inventory–Adolescent (MMPI–A)*, the *High School Personality Questionnaire*, the *Guilford-Zimmerman Temperament Survey*, the *Anxiety Scales for Children and Adults*, and the *Millon Adolescent Personality Inventory*. Although these instruments are often used with children, there are problems associated with this type of assessment.

First, there is the possibility of faking one's answers. Although personality testing should be done with the aim of helping a child, some children may be afraid to admit to feelings or thoughts that they perceive as socially unacceptable or undesirable. Furthermore, even if there is not a conscious effort at faking a score, a child may not have the insight needed to honestly answer all of the items. Consider, for example, the items included in Figure 6.1. Not only may a child be reluctant to give a candid answer to some items, particularly knowing that the answer may be seen by his or her teacher, but the child may really not know the answer.

On many self-report instruments, there is also the possibility of a response set. As described in the context of interest inventories in Chapter 5, a response set is a tendency to respond to all of the items in similar fashion, regardless of the actual question. For example, students may say "yes" to everything, say "no" to everything, be noncommittal, or consistently give what is perceived to be the socially desirable response. For this reason, instruments such as the *MMPI–A* include scales that are designed to detect specific response sets. If a response set is detected, the score is invalidated.

Other instruments, such as the *Gordon Personal Profile–Inventory*, attempt to overcome the problem with a forced-choice format. On this and similar instruments, as illustrated in Figure 6.1, students are not only required to say whether an item describes them, but also to indicate which of a group of four items that are equally socially desirable is most like them and which is least like them. Thus, even if all four items are undesirable, the student is forced to select one that best describes him or her; the student doesn't have the choice of saying that none of them apply. Even these precautions, however, do not guarantee the validity of the scores. There is often resistance to this type of a scale and students may respond randomly or, for example, always say that the first descriptor is most like them and the last is least like them.

In addition to self-report inventories, there are also instruments that are used by others to rate a child. Particularly in the lower grades, a parent or teacher may be requested to describe the child. There are also a number of instruments that are completed by both the child and by others. Typical of

Figure 6.1
Sample Items from the *Minnesota Multiphasic Personality*
Inventory–Adolescent (MMPI–A)

```
        Examinees are to answer True or False to each item.


  I enjoy detective or mystery stories.

  There seems to be a lump in my throat most of the time.

  My teachers have it in for me.

  I have sometimes stolen things.

  I get angry sometimes.

  My parents do not really love me.

  I have nightmares every few nights.

  Most people think they can depend on me.

  I do the things I am supposed to do around home.

  I enjoy using marijuana.

  I have a close friend whom I can share secrets with.
```

Minnesota Multiphasic Personality Inventory–Adolescent (MMPI–A). Copyright © the
   Regents of the University of Minnesota 1942, 1943 (renewed 1970), 1992. Reproduced
   by permission of the publisher.

"Minnesota Multiphasic Personality Inventory–Adolescent" and "MMPI–A" are trademarks
   owned by the University of Minnesota.

these are the *Behavior Rating Profile*, which is completed by the student
and by the parent, the teacher, and peers; the *Social-Emotional Dimension
Scale*, which may be used by teachers, counselors, and psychologists; and
the *Walker-McConnell Scale of Social Competence and School Adjustment*,
which is completed by a teacher who has observed a child over a period of
time.

   When others are reporting on the behavior of a child, of course, they can
only report on observed behavior. Although they can infer a child's feelings,
they really don't know how a child felt in a particular situation or why a
child behaved in a specific way. Also, any one person sees only a limited
portion of a child's behavior and interactions with others, which is why
some of these instruments ask for reports from a variety of other individuals.

It must also be kept in mind that the ratings may be colored by the raters' biases and preconceptions as well as by incomplete or distorted recollections. When rating a child, the rater usually has to think back and recollect how a child typically behaves. What an individual recollects, and the interpretation that is later put on these recollections, is often shaped by later experiences. As with self-ratings, then, ratings by others also raise serious questions of validity and reliability.

Projective Techniques

Projective techniques are methods of assessment in which personality characteristics are inferred from the way an individual responds to vague or ambiguous tasks. An individual may be asked, for example, to describe what is seen in an inkblot, to tell a story about a picture, to draw a figure, or to provide the ending for an incomplete sentence. There are no correct or incorrect responses to these tasks, but different personality characteristics are inferred from different types of responses.

Typical of these techniques are the *Rotter Incomplete Sentences Blank*; the *Draw A Person procedure*; the *Rorschach Technique* and the *Holtzman Inkblot Technique*, both of which require youngsters to describe what they see in an inkblot; and the *Thematic Apperception Test* and the *Children's Apperception Technique*, which both require the examinee to make up stories about a series of pictures. The use of these techniques is reserved for professionals trained in their administration and scoring. It is highly unusual for them to be given in cases where problems are not suspected.

One advantage of projective techniques is that, since most people don't know how their responses are being interpreted, it is difficult to fake a response. Furthermore, someone who might be hesitant or unable to reveal personal feelings in response to direct questions is more likely to reveal them when engaged in the vague and ambiguous tasks called for in this type of test.

Although there is a trend toward more systematic interpretation of some of the projective techniques, there is still considerable concern about their validity and reliability. As with all personality tests, these tests should be part of a more complete evaluation of a child, and the scores should be viewed as supplemental to other sources of information in explaining a child's behavior.

It is more difficult to establish the validity and reliability of personality tests than it is for achievement and aptitude tests, and these measures should always be interpreted with caution. Scores should be interpreted by trained professionals and should never be viewed as providing a definitive diagnosis of a problem in the absence of other supporting information about the child. Personality tests do not provide infallible diagnoses and must always be interpreted in the context of everything else that is known about a child.

ASSESSMENT OF ATTITUDES

Similar to personality tests are attitude tests, which assess an individual's dispositions or reactions toward other individuals, objects, or events. Although attitude surveys are sometimes used in conjunction with personality tests in order to gain insight into a child's behavior, attitude assessment is more often used in the schools to evaluate curriculum or to assess the outlook of a class rather than that of a particular child. Before starting a unit on Native Americans, for example, a teacher might want to determine the preexisting attitudes of the class toward this population. Alternatively, a high school administration may want to assess whether changes in the science curriculum have resulted in more positive attitudes toward science.

Although some published attitude scales are available, such as the *Survey of Study Habits and Attitudes*, which measures attitudes toward school activities, many of the attitude scales administered in the schools are locally constructed and lack evidence of reliability and validity. They are useful for obtaining a general sense of the views of a group, but great care must be taken in interpreting the scores.

The most commonly used type of attitude scale, called a summated rating scale, consists of several statements to which students must indicate their agreement or disagreement. The items illustrated in Figure 6.2 are typical of this type of scale. Usually, students will be asked to indicate their degree of agreement on either a five-value scale, such as the one illustrated, or on a seven-value scale. The response format may vary; instead of circling their response, students may sometimes be asked to write in a number or a letter representing their degree of agreement or may be asked to place a check or an X at the appropriate point on a graphic scale. Regardless of the format, the score is obtained by summing the values assigned to the student's response to each of the items.

Summated rating scales, however, should include items that reflect both positive and negative attitudes. When the item scores are summed, the score values are reversed for the negative items. On the scale illustrated in Figure 6.2, for example, a score value of 5 would be assigned to items #2, #3, and #5 in cases where the student circled a value of 1. Thus, students who were

Figure 6.2
A Summated Rating Scale

Attitudes Toward Coeducational Teams

Mark your agreement to each of the following statements by circling:

    1, if you strongly disagree with the statement;
    2, if you mildly disagree with the statement;
    3, if you neither agree nor disagree;
    4, if you mildly agree with the statement;
    5, if you strongly agree with the statement.

1.	I would be more likely to join a team if boys and girls were on the same team than if there were different teams for boys and girls.	1	2	3	4	5
2.	I would never join a team that had both boys and girls.	1	2	3	4	5
3.	Boys and girls would distract each other from playing well if they were on the same team.	1	2	3	4	5
4.	I would like to be on a team that had both boys and girls.	1	2	3	4	5
5.	It's OK for boys and girls to be on the same debate team but not an athletic team.	1	2	3	4	5
6.	Boys and girls would learn to get along better with each other if they played on teams together.	1	2	3	4	5

positively disposed toward coeducational teams would have high scores, and those who were negatively disposed would have low scores.

Both positive and negative items are included on this type of scale to reduce the response set of acquiescence. The same response sets that affect the scores on interest inventories and personality tests also affect the scores on attitude scales. Although including both positive and negative items may not entirely eliminate the set for acquiescence, this practice makes it less likely for a student to routinely give the same response to every item. An attempt should also be made to equate both positive and negative items for social desirability, although it is very difficult to eliminate either the tendency to give the socially desirable response or the ability to fake one's responses.

Another problem with this type of scale is that it is not always clear what the middle score value represents. When students circle 3, does it mean that they are indifferent—neither positive nor negative—toward that statement, or does it mean that they aren't sure about how they feel? Additionally, students do not always agree on what it means to strongly disagree: what one student may characterize as strong agreement may be another student's mild agreement.

Some of these problems are dealt with by the use of different types of scales. On some of these scales students are given pairs of statements and, within each pair, are asked to choose the statement that best reflects their feelings. On others they are asked to rank a set of statements in order of their agreement with each statement or to indicate where they would place a statement on a continuum between two adjectives. In measuring attitudes toward mathematics, for example, a student might be asked to indicate where mathematics would fall on the following graphic scale:

GOOD ____ ____ ____ ____ ____ ____ ____ BAD
          1   2   3   4   5   6   7

Regardless of the form of the scale, however, attitude assessment is problematic. Aside from the fact that the reliability and validity of these instruments tend to be low, attitude scales simply indicate what individuals are willing to say, not necessarily how they will behave. Even when responses are not consciously faked, there may be little correspondence between what someone says they will do and how they will behave in an actual situation. Furthermore, norms are rarely available, making it difficult to establish the meaning of different scores. On a scale of attitudes toward mathematics where the highest possible score is 50, what does a score of 40 mean? Do only college mathematics majors get scores this high? Or do most high school students score in this range?

Attitude assessment can supplement the information provided by aptitude, achievement, and personality tests and can contribute to an understanding of a child's behavior. Attitude assessment is also useful in assessing the views of different groups of youngsters and the effects of curriculum change. Be cautioned, however; it is often not clear exactly what the score on an attitude scale means or whether the score on an attitude scale corresponds to observable behavior in an analogous situation.

Chapter 7

Special Tests for Special Situations

Daryl is a six-year-old who gets along well with other children, has quickly adapted to the routines of his first grade class, and appears eager to learn. His physical development has been normal, and his performance on the screening test that was administered when he registered for kindergarten indicated normal to above-average intelligence. He seems to be having difficulty in learning to read, however, and his teacher has noticed that he doesn't always seem to understand or remember the directions given for different activities.

In a situation such as this, a learning disability may be suspected and the child may be referred for further testing. This chapter will focus on those tests that may be given to diagnose problems associated with various types of learning disabilities and/or neurological impairment, as well as some of the tests that are used to assess intellectual functioning in children with disabilities. It will not deal with issues related to the diagnosis of severe mental retardation or physical disabilities.

At this point, it should be noted that the Education for All Handicapped Children Act (Public Law 94-142), which was enacted in 1975 (and amended in 1990 to be designated the Individuals with Disabilities Education Act), includes several provisions regarding the identification of children with disabilities and the assessment of their scholastic aptitude and achievement. The purpose of PL 94-142 was to assure all children with disabilities "a free appropriate public education which emphasizes special education and related services designed to meet their unique needs, to assure that the rights of children with disabilities and their guardians are protected, to assist States and localities to provide for the education of all children with disabilities, and to assess and assure the effectiveness of efforts to educate children with disabilities."[1] The children covered by the Act are those "(i) with mental retardation, hearing impairments including deafness, speech impairments, visual impairments including blindness, serious emotional disturbance, orthopedic impairments, autism, other health impairments, or specific learning disabilities; and (ii) who, by reason thereof, need special education and related services."[2] The Act was not intended to cover "children whose learning problems are caused by environmental, cultural or economic disadvantage" nor those who are "slow learners."[3]

Although many of the disabilities included in PL 94-142 are clearly identifiable, the identification of children with learning disabilities as well as those who are educable mentally retarded and/or severely emotionally disturbed is less clear cut. The difficulties involved in making these classifications are even more pronounced when assessing children from minority groups or those with language difficulties. Cases have been cited in which children from minority groups were identified as having handicapping conditions and placed in classes for the mentally retarded when, in fact, they did not have such conditions. These cases led to particular concern about the appropriate assessment of the learning needs of children whose disabilities or whose cultural or language background may compromise the validity of normal testing procedures.

To address these problems and to provide for the appropriate assessment of such children, provisions were included in PL 94-142 "to assure that the testing and evaluation materials utilized for the purposes of evaluation and placement of handicapped children will be selected and administered so as not to be racially or culturally discriminatory."[4] The rules and regulations regarding the implementation of the Act provide that:

(a) Tests and other evaluation materials:

(1) Are provided and administered in the child's native language or other mode of communication (e.g., braille or sign language), unless it is clearly not feasible to do so;

(2) Have been validated for the specific purpose for which they are used; and

(3) Are administered by trained personnel in conformance with instructions provided by their producer;

(b) Tests and other evaluation materials include those tailored to assess specific areas of educational need and not merely those which are designed to provide a single general intelligence quotient;

(c) Tests are selected and administered so as best to ensure that when a test is administered to a child with impaired sensory, manual or speaking skills, the test results accurately reflect the child's aptitude or achievement level or whatever other factors the test purports to measure, rather than reflecting the child's impaired sensory, manual or spelling skills (except where those skills are the factors which the test purports to measure).

(d) No single procedure is used as the sole criterion for determining an appropriate educational program for a child; and

(e) The evaluation is made by a multidisciplinary team or group of persons, including at least one teacher or other specialist with knowledge in the area of suspected disability.

(f) The child is assessed in all areas related to the suspected disability, including, where appropriate, health, vision, hearing, social and emotional status, general intelligence, academic performance, communicative status, and motor abilities.[5]

These regulations reflect good assessment practice and must be followed both when identifying a child as having a disability and when assessing the achievement and aptitude of children already identified as such. In these situations, as in any evaluation procedure, no one test score should be taken as infallible, the information provided by any measurement instrument should be considered in the context of other information known about the child, and attention must be paid to the validity and reliability of the instruments used. It should be recognized, however, that although following these procedures will help reduce measurement error, it will not be eliminated.

THE ASSESSMENT OF LEARNING DISABILITIES

The designation of a child as learning disabled implies neurological problems that are manifest in circumscribed learning difficulties. There has been little success, however, in connecting particular learning problems with specific neurological impairments. PL 94-142 defines a specific learning disability as "a disorder in one or more of the basic psychological processes involved in understanding or in using language, spoken or written, which may manifest itself in an imperfect ability to listen, think, speak, read, write, spell or to do mathematical calculations. The term includes such conditions as perceptual handicaps, brain injury, minimal brain disfunction, dyslexia, and developmental aphasia. The term does not include children who have learning problems which are primarily the result of visual, hearing, or motor handicaps, or mental retardation, or of environmental, cultural, or economic disadvantage."[6]

In practice, the feature that distinguishes the designation of learning disabled from that of educable mentally retarded is a discrepancy between performance on scholastic aptitude tests and achievement in specific academic areas. A child classified as educable mentally retarded will demonstrate consistently below average performance on scholastic aptitude tests as well as on achievement tests in most school subjects; a child classified as learning disabled, on the other hand, will demonstrate average or above-average performance on scholastic aptitude tests. The child classified as learning disabled may also perform well on some achievement measures, but there will be a significant discrepancy between the aptitude test performance and achievement in specific areas.

In youngsters who otherwise exhibit normal abilities, poor performance in one of the following areas may be attributed to a learning disability: oral or written expression, listening comprehension, reading, mathematics, and spelling. Where a learning disability is suspected, the child is likely to be referred for diagnostic testing. The purpose of the testing is to confirm whether or not a problem exists and, if so, to diagnose the specific areas of strength and weakness.

A child referred for further diagnosis will usually be given an individually administered scholastic aptitude test. In addition to the tests mentioned in Chapter 5, tests such as the *McCarthy Scales of Children's Abilities* may be administered, which not only provide an overall measure of scholastic aptitude but also include subscales that are particularly useful in identifying specific learning disabilities. In addition to a general cognitive scale, the *McCarthy Scales of Children's Abilities* includes a verbal scale, a quantitative scale, a memory scale, a perceptual-performance scale, and a motor scale.

If difficulties have been noted in mathematics, reading, or spelling, regular achievement tests in these areas are also likely to be administered. It is likely, however, that rather than administering one of the achievement batteries that are regularly given to all students in the school, tests will be selected that have more items focusing on the specific problem area.

Additionally, an individually administered achievement test may be given that enables the psychologist to get a better understanding of the processes a child uses in arriving at an answer. Often used for this purpose are tests such as the *Wide-Range Achievement Test–Revised (WRAT–R)*, the *Basic Achievement Skills Individual Screener (BASIS)*, the *Test of Academic Performance*, the *Multilevel Academic Survey Tests*, the *Sequential Assessment of Mathematics Inventories–Standardized Inventory (SAMI)*, the *Peabody Individual Achievement Test–Revised (PIAT–R)*, the *KeyMath Revised*, the *Kaufman Test of Educational Achievement*, and the *Wechsler Individual Achievement Test (WAIT)*.

These tests assess achievement in basic areas of school learning and enable the psychologist to better diagnose a youngster's strengths and weaknesses. When these tests reveal weaknesses that might stem from perceptual or other neurological problems or, perhaps, delayed speech and language development, further testing is likely to be done in these areas. Such testing is more likely to be carried out in a clinical environment, however, than in the school. Typical of the tests used for this purpose are: the *Bender Visual Motor Gestalt Test*, which assesses visual perception; the *Benton Visual Retention Test*, which assesses visual perception and visual memory; the *Quick Neurological Screening Test*, which assesses visual and auditory perception, as well as attention, balance, motor development and sequencing, and spatial organization; the *Wide-Range Assessment of Memory and Learning*, which assesses both verbal and visual memory; the *California Verbal Learning Test for Children* and the *Children's Auditory Verbal Learning Test*, both of which test long- and short-term memory; the *Children's Category Test*, which tests concept formation, memory, and learning from experience; the *Wisconsin Card Sorting Test*, which requires examinees to sort cards according to different criteria and which claims to identify lesions in the brain's frontal lobes; the *Bader Test of Reading-Spelling Patterns*, which identifies different types of reading disabilities; and the *Test of Language Development (TOLD)*, which assesses different aspects of spoken language at the primary and intermediate levels.

The purpose of these tests is to identify and explain the particular learning problems that prompted the initial referral. If neurological problems are suspected, the child may be referred to a neurologist for further examination. In other cases, these tests may aid in formulating a plan for remediation or for helping the child to compensate for the problem.

ASSESSING COGNITIVE FUNCTIONING IN CHILDREN WITH DISABILITIES

The usual paper-and-pencil aptitude and achievement tests may not always be appropriate for children with disabilities. Those with some physical disabilities may not be able to hear or see oral or written directions or test items, and those with motor problems may have difficulty in writing their answers. Additionally, children with learning disabilities might have a language or perceptual problem that interferes with their ability to take the test. When such is the case, tests and testing procedures should be used that compensate for the disability.

The Use of Modified Testing Procedures

In some cases, regular tests will be used with modified test procedures. Written instructions or test items, for example, may be read to the examinee; answers may be given orally instead of written; or time limits may be extended. Additionally, some examinations come in Braille or large-type editions. In all of these instances, however, there are problems in using regular norms; regular norms reflect the performance of students taking the test under standard conditions, and we do not know how they would perform under modified conditions. Consider, for example, a high school student who, because of a physical disability, is administered the *SAT I: Reasoning Test* orally and without time limits. It does not seem fair to hold a student in such a situation to the normal time limits; it takes more time to have the items read aloud than to read them to oneself, and it may also be more difficult to comprehend the items when they are administered in this way. It is certainly more difficult to go back and reread parts that were not at first absorbed or were confusing. But how much additional time is needed? And to what extent does orally reading the items affect their difficulty? These questions have not been answered, making it very difficult to interpret the score. With tests such as the *SAT I*, the conditions of testing are reported along with the score. Although this practice alerts those who are using the scores to interpret them with care, the scores are not directly comparable to those obtained by students taking the test under standard conditions. Score interpretation is limited; when a test is taken under modified conditions, norm-referenced scores do not have the same meaning as they do when the test is administered under standard procedures.

Tests Designed to Compensate for Disabilities

Another approach to assessing children with disabilities is to use tests that have been specifically designed to compensate for their disabilities. The *Peabody Picture Vocabulary Test–Revised (PPVT–R)*, for example, a measure of listening vocabulary that does not require any reading or writing, is sometimes used to assess scholastic aptitude; the test items are pictures and the examinee responds by pointing. The *Test of Nonverbal Intelligence– 2 (TONI–2)* is also used to assess intelligence and reasoning abilities in children who have language problems. The *Matrix Analogies Test*, as well as the other nonverbal tests mentioned in Chapter 5, are also used in this situation. For children who are hearing disabled, special tests such as the *Test of Early Reading Ability–Deaf or Hard of Hearing*, the *Rhode Island Test of Language Structure*, and the *Carolina Picture Vocabulary Test* may be used to assess reading and language skills.

In assessing children with disabilities, it should be remembered that PL 94-142 requires non-discriminatory testing in the child's native language. In addition to the language-free or culture-fair tests used for this purpose, there are also foreign language versions of several popular tests. It should be noted, however, that simply translating a test into another language does not make the test culture-fair. Furthermore, the English-language norms are not applicable to a test translated into a foreign language. One approach to this problem has been the development of the System of Multicultural Pluralistic Assessment (SOMPA) described in Chapter 5. SOMPA is de-signed to take language and cultural differences into account in estimating a child's cognitive, perceptual, and psychomotor abilities and may be used with children with disabilities from different cultural backgrounds.

It must be noted, however, that there are still serious problems associated with the assessment of children with disabilities. When modified testing procedures are used, the interpretation of norm-referenced scores becomes questionable and, although tests are available that compensate for some disabilities, concerns have been raised about the validity of these tests. As mentioned in Chapter 5, language-free and culture-fair scholastic aptitude tests are not as predictive of school performance as those that are more highly verbal. Furthermore, appropriate norms are not generally available for children with different disabilities.

In assessing children with disabilities, then, it is very important to consider a variety of different sources of information. This information should include not only formal test scores but the observations of parents and classroom teachers, as well as those of other professionals who work with the child. Even then there may be differences of opinion as to the evaluation and, in fact, the rules and regulations regarding PL 94-142 include provisions for parents to obtain an independent educational evaluation of their child. Although the enactment of PL 94-142 has focused attention on the need to develop and use non-discriminatory assessment procedures, much work remains to be done in refining the validity and reliability of the measurement instruments and procedures used.

NOTES

1. Education for All Handicapped Children Act of 1975, §601, 20 U.S.C. §1401 (1975).

2. Education for All Handicapped Children Act of 1975, 20 U.S.C. §1401 (1975, as amended 1990).

3. Senate Report No. 94-168, p. 10 (1975).

4. Education for All Handicapped Children Act of 1975, §612, 20 U.S.C. §1401 (1975).

5. Rules and Regulations. (1977, August 23). *Federal Register.* p. 42496, §121a.531.

6. Education for All Handicapped Children Act of 1975, 20 U.S.C. §1401 (1975, as amended 1990).

Chapter 8

What Does the Score Tell You?

A test score, as we have seen, describes how your child performed on a particular set of test items at a particular time. What the score tells you about that performance depends upon both the nature of the test and the form in which the score is reported.

This chapter will introduce you to the different types of scores that are used to report test performance and indicate the type of information they provide. In subsequent chapters we will look more closely at the interpretation of each particular type of score. In this chapter, however, we will focus on the distinction between norm-referenced and criterion-referenced scores, as well as the broader questions that ought to be raised in order to more fully understand the information that test scores provide.

Before looking at the different types of scores, however, it must be emphasized that any test score simply describes a particular performance at a particular time, and it may or may not be indicative of the child's ability. Just as a top-seeded tennis player may have an "off" day and miss some easy shots, a child may have an "off" day and miss some easy items on a test. It isn't until we see a pattern of performance that we can make a reasonable judgment about the representativeness of a particular test score.

A score of 70% on an arithmetic test, for example, would be seen quite differently for a child who is known to be gifted in mathematics than it would be for a child who usually has difficulty in computation. What would the score of 70% mean for the child who is mathematically gifted? Has the child's ability declined? Does the 70% represent the child's true degree of mastery of the material that was tested? Is the score telling us that the child has stopped doing the homework and has fallen behind in the work? Or did a stomachache prevent the child from concentrating on the test? Was the test unusually difficult? Or was it that the test was so poorly constructed that the child couldn't figure out what the teacher was asking?

A test score doesn't answer these questions. It doesn't even ask them. A test score is simply a description of one particular performance. In order to properly interpret that score, you must not only understand what the number means, but also consider the outside factors that may have contributed to that performance.

Sometimes, people throw out the baby with the bath water; they totally disregard test scores because the scores aren't as infallible as one might hope. Test scores do provide valuable information, but no score is a perfect measure of a child's ability. In order to best interpret what a particular score is telling you, the score must be put in context. Is this score typical of the child's performance in the area tested? Does it match with what the teacher observes in class and the parents' perception of the child's ability? Are there any extenuating circumstances that might be affecting the child's perform-ance? The answers to these questions are as important to interpreting the score as is an understanding of what the number means.

The score on a test is a measure in the same way that a reading on your bathroom scale is a measure. You would not disregard all measures of your weight because some scales are less accurate than others, because your weight is higher than you would like, because you ate too much last night, or because you are wearing more clothes today than yesterday. Instead, you would try to take these factors into account. In the same way, these outside factors must also be considered in interpreting the meaning of a test score.

Of course, even after taking these factors into account, you must then know whether the reading on the scale was in pounds or kilograms, and you must know what these different measures mean. In the same way, you must also know whether a test score is a raw score, an age or a grade score, a rank or a standard score. Let us look, then, at the different types of test scores and what they tell you about a child's performance.

THE MAJOR TYPES OF TEST SCORES

When a child has taken a test, the score may be reported in several different forms. Sometimes you may be told the raw score, which is the number of items answered correctly, or you may be given the percentage of items correct. At other times, a child's performance may be reported as an age or grade score, a rank, a percentile rank, or one of a group of scores, such as IQ scores and stanines, called standard scores.

These different types of scores can be divided into two broad categories:

(1) Criterion-referenced scores, which tell you the degree to which a child has mastered the material that was tested, or

(2) Norm-referenced scores, which tell you how the child compares to other children on the tasks included on the test.

If the test is criterion-referenced, or designed to determine the degree to which a particular subject unit has been mastered, the score is likely to be reported as either the number or the percentage of items correct. Age and grade scores, percentile ranks, and standard scores, on the other hand, fall into the category of norm-referenced scores.

Criterion-referenced and norm-referenced scores provide you with very different information about a child's performance. Each type of information is important and, in fact, both types of scores are often reported on standardized tests.

Criterion-Referenced Testing: Testing for Mastery

Criterion-referenced tests are designed to tell you the proficiencies or skills a child has mastered. The score on a criterion-referenced test is independent of the performance of the other children who were tested. These scores will not tell you how a child's performance compares to the performance of other children. They won't tell you whether the child is at the top of the class or at the bottom, or whether the child is performing above or below grade level. Regardless of anyone else's performance, a criterion-referenced score will simply tell you whether or not the child displayed proficiency at the particular skills that were tested.

Mastery and Minimum Competency Tests

Most criterion-referenced tests are referred to as mastery tests. A specified level of performance on the test is designated as the criterion of mastery, and children who score above that criterion are said to have mastered the material that was tested. Assume, for example, that a score of 80% is designated as the criterion of mastery on a test designed to measure proficiency at subtraction of double-digit numbers. If a child could answer 90% of the problems correctly, the child would have demonstrated mastery in subtracting double-digit numbers. Similarly, a child with a score of 60%, which is below the criterion of mastery, would be said not to have mastered the skill in question.

On this type of a test, each child's performance is compared to the criterion of mastery rather than to the performance of other children. It is possible for every child in the class to attain mastery or, on the other hand, for every child to fail to attain mastery. Mastery tests are not designed to discriminate among children with varied levels of ability, but simply to differentiate those who have mastered the material from those who have not. The score on a mastery test, therefore, will not necessarily tell you how well a child has mastered the work, but merely whether or not your child has mastered the competencies that differentiate masters from non-masters. Some children may have progressed far beyond the competencies tested, while others may have just squeaked through. Children at both levels of performance will be classified as masters. Similarly, children who are just barely below the criterion for mastery, as well as those who show the most minimal competence will be classified as non-masters.

Some criterion-referenced tests are called minimum competency tests. These tests assess the basic skills that students must master in order to be considered minimally competent in a subject area. In some states there are minimum competency tests in a variety of subjects that students must pass in order to receive a high school diploma. Students who score at or above the criterion of mastery on these tests may receive the diploma, regardless of how far above the criterion they score. Similarly, students who fall below the criterion for mastery may not receive the diploma, even if they miss it by only one or two points.

Furthermore, even those students who receive very high grades on these tests cannot be assumed to have more than very minimal competence because the tests are, in fact, designed to measure only the most minimal competencies in the subject tested. A minimum competency test in arithmetic, for example, does not include complex problems that involve skills beyond the level of minimum competence. Instead, the content of the test items is such that only those skills designated as the minimum competencies are required in order to get the items right. Thus, a student who was very proficient in those minimum skills, but who lacked the more advanced skills, would be likely to get the same top score as a youngster who had mastered skills far beyond the level of minimum competency.

Consider, for example, a simple arithmetic test designed to assess competency in the addition of two single-digit numbers. If the test included twenty problems such as 3+4=? and 5+1=?, a second-grader who was proficient in addition could obtain the same score as a professor with a Ph.D. in mathematics. This occurrence would certainly not mean that the second-grader was as proficient in mathematics as the professor, but that both were equally proficient on the minimal competencies tested. Both the second-grader and the professor would have demonstrated mastery of the skill of adding of two single-digit numbers.

Not all criterion-referenced tests, however, fall into the category of mastery or minimum competency tests. Some criterion-referenced tests do distinguish among different levels of competency. Consider, for example, the typical classroom test. A teacher may give a twenty item arithmetic test on which a score of 65%, or 13 items correct, is designated the criterion of mastery or the "passing grade." Most classroom tests, however, test more than minimum competencies. The typical classroom test has some items that require more complex skills and reasoning than would be required to demonstrate only minimum competency, and those students who have mastered these more complex skills do attain higher scores on the test. In order to get a 90% on the test, for example, a student may have had to demonstrate a number of skills beyond those required to simply pass the test.

These tests do differentiate among students with different levels of mastery. They are still considered to be criterion-referenced tests, however, because students are compared to a criterion of performance rather than to other students. A student with a 90% on the test has correctly answered 90% of the items on the test, and that score would remain the same regardless of the scores of any other youngsters in the class. The score of 90% represents the degree to which the child has mastered the material that was tested, and it is possible for all the children to receive scores of 90% if all have mastered the material to the same extent.

It should be pointed out, however, that the scores on a criterion-referenced test are easier to interpret when the test is limited to a clearly defined and limited set of tasks relating to a particular skill. As the subject area tested becomes broader and more general, it becomes harder to relate the score to the particular skills a child has mastered. That is not to say that more complex skills, or competencies above the level of minimum competency, should not be tested. Indeed, one of the criticisms of testing is that many tests are already too limited in the skills that they assess. When testing broad areas of achievement, however, we could better diagnose a child's strengths and weaknesses if separate scores were provided on the separate skills that go into each unit.

Assume, for example, that a child has a score of 80% on a third grade arithmetic test on which 65% is the criterion of mastery. This information would tell you that the child has mastered the general area of third grade arithmetic, but not which skills have or have not been mastered. If, on the other hand, separate scores were provided on computational skills in addition, subtraction, multiplication, and division, on problem-solving and application skills, and on number theory, and a criterion of mastery was provided for each of these sections, the information provided would be much more meaningful. Not only would you know that the child had mastered third grade arithmetic, but you would know just which skills had been mastered, and in which areas the child might be in need of further help. Furthermore, assuming that each of these sections had problems requiring minimum competencies as well as some requiring a higher level of proficiency, you would know that a high score in a particular area would mean that your child had acquired higher level skills in that particular area.

Setting the Criterion of Mastery

The idea of criterion-referenced scores is very appealing, and criterion-referenced testing is becoming more widespread. Ideally, these scores give us an absolute measure of the skills that children have mastered. In actual practice, however, it is quite obvious that mastery is not always that easy to define and that the criteria for mastery are often arbitrary. To fully understand what these scores mean, then, you need more information than the score itself. You have to know exactly which skills were being measured, and you have to know how the criterion for mastery was set.

Consider, for example, a skill such as subtracting double-digit numbers. How would we know whether or not this skill was mastered? We would probably agree that we should give the child some problems in which double-digit subtraction was required. But how many problems would be adequate? And how many must the child get right in order for us to agree that the skill had indeed been mastered?

We might be wary if the arithmetic test had only a single problem, or even three or four. After all, a child might do fine on problems such as

$$
\begin{array}{cccccc}
44 & 98 & 37 & & 14 \\
-22 & -63 & -20 & \text{and} & -12 \\
\end{array}
$$

but might not know how to handle problems such as

$$
\begin{array}{ccccc}
60 & 73 & & 31 \\
-48 & -67 & \text{or} & -19 \\
\end{array}
$$

We would want to be sure that enough problems were asked so that the domain of double-digit subtraction problems was adequately represented. We would want to make sure, for example, that there were some problems that involved "borrowing" and others that involved subtracting from a number with a zero. We might disagree, however, on just exactly how many problems that would be.

Even if we agreed that the test adequately represented the domain of double-digit subtraction, however, we would still have to determine what level of performance would be indicative of mastery. We would probably agree that a child who had a score of 100% on 50 double-digit subtraction problems had mastered this skill. But what about the child with 48 items correct? If 100% were set as the criterion for mastery, what would happen to all those children who had truly mastered the skill but made careless mistakes? Or those who meant to write a "2," but whose "2" looked more like a "7"? Since we have to leave some room for error, the criterion for mastery would not be set at 100%. But where, then, do we draw the line?

At the present time, there is no one agreed-upon method of setting an appropriate criterion of mastery. On many tests, particularly teacher-made classroom tests, the criterion is purely arbitrary. On other tests, the criterion is based on an analysis of the subsequent performance of children who had previously taken the test. In such cases, the criterion for mastery would be the score that was found to best distinguish between those youngsters who could successfully move on to other units and those who were not yet ready to do so.

When you receive scores on a mastery test, it is appropriate to ask how the criterion for mastery was set. If you feel that a child does not truly understand the work, but the child's grades are well above the mastery level, it may very well be that the criterion is inappropriately low. Similarly, if a child is working with difficult material and apparently understands the work, but is below the level of mastery, the criterion may be too high.

Consider, for example, the typical teacher-made test in the secondary schools. Let's say we have a tenth grade mathematics class in which a grade of 65% on the final examination has been set as the "passing" grade. Essentially, we are saying that a grade of 65% is the criterion for mastery. Students who obtain grades of 65% or better are assumed to have mastered the minimum skills required for us to say that they have mastered tenth grade mathematics. But why 65%? What makes 65% the appropriate criterion? In too many cases, unfortunately, the decision is based purely on convention and has no empirical basis. No analysis is done to determine exactly which skills would be necessary to obtain a score of 65%, or whether the score could be obtained by doing very well on several peripheral areas and not having mastered some of the essential skills needed for successful progress in subsequent courses.

Accounting for the Difficulty of the Test

Another issue here is the difficulty of the test. We have all had the experience where one teacher's tests are very easy and another's are very hard, and the students in one class therefore have higher grades than in the other. What if David is in the class with the easier teacher and has a 92% on this term's final examination as opposed to an 84% on last term's final. Is David doing better in math? His grade is certainly higher, but what does it mean? David has mastered more of what was on this term's test than what was on last term's test, but maybe that is because this term's test was too easy. He may have actually mastered more of the work in the previous year. In fact, the grade of 84% could have been higher than the grades received by 90% of the students in last year's class, while the grade of 92 may be better than the grades received by only 85% of the students in this year's class. How do we know for sure? We don't! Very often, however, a look at how other children did can give us a clue as to the appropriateness of the test.

If we have a typical class in which the youngsters appear to be successful in learning the work and doing the assignments, but everyone is doing very poorly on the tests, there is reason to suspect that the tests are too difficult. Tests can be inappropriately difficult for many reasons. The items can be so poorly stated that even youngsters who actually knew the material didn't realize what was being asked. Or the items could require trivial discriminations or touch on material that wasn't covered.

Where you suspect that it is the test and not the child's mastery of the material that is causing the low grade, it is useful to look at the child's relative performance. Here is a situation where norm-referenced scores would provide useful information. If the child is usually in the upper 10% of the class, and usually gets grades in the 90s, scores in the 70s might be a source of concern. The question, then, is whether the child is falling down, or whether the testing is such that everyone in the class is scoring lower than usual. If the child is still in the top 10% of the class, it means that the child is still at the same relative level of performance but that everyone is doing more poorly on the tests.

What you don't know, however, is whether it is just the test that is difficult or whether the youngsters are in fact finding the work more difficult. It may be that the work itself is very difficult to master. You may then question whether the difficulty is because of the nature of the material or whether it is because the teacher is not very good at explaining the concepts involved. You can see the problem here. Unfortunately, there is no one way to find a definitive answer to these questions. The answers must be sought through an analyses of the many factors that can influence the score on a test.

Factors Related to Validity and Reliability

Consideration must be given to personal factors that might temporarily affect performance, factors related to the nature of the material being tested and the way in which the skills were taught, factors unique to the particular testing situation, and factors relating to the test. As with any test, before the score can be interpreted, you must have some idea as to the validity and reliability of the scores.

A criterion-referenced test must have content validity. That is, the content of the test items must directly correspond to the knowledge and abilities that are inherent in the skill being assessed. A criterion-referenced test must also show evidence of being reliable. Since scores on criterion-referenced tests may not be as spread out as on other tests, many of the traditional measures of reliability cannot be used to assess the reliability of these tests. Nevertheless, similar questions can be asked. For example, do testings with an equal number of equivalent but different problems yield comparable results? Are the same children who are classified as "masters" on one form of the test similarly classified on another form? As with any test, we want to know whether the score is accurate before we start to interpret its meaning.

As you can see then, a test score is merely a measure of performance on a particular measuring instrument at a particular time, and the interpretation of that score must take into account myriad factors. The score on a criterion-referenced test ostensibly tells you whether or not the particular skill being tested was mastered, but the interpretation of any test score must go hand in hand with an evaluation of the test itself and the many factors that may have influenced a child's performance on that test.

These same factors must also be considered when interpreting norm-referenced scores. As you will see, however, norm-referenced scores provide very different information about a child's performance.

Norm-Referenced Testing: Measuring Relative Performance

In contrast to the score on a criterion-referenced test, which tells you what skills a child has mastered, the score on a norm-referenced test tells you how a child's performance compares to that of other children.

On a norm-referenced test, the raw score may be misleading. Assume, for example, that Allison received the following scores on an arithmetic and a reading test:

Raw Scores on a Reading and Arithmetic Test

Arithmetic Score	*Reading Score*
80	80

As you can see, the raw scores were the same. But does that mean that Allison is performing at the same relative level in both subjects? You cannot draw that conclusion from the information presented. Even though the scores appear to be the same, she may have scored above more of the other children on the arithmetic test than on the reading test.

Consider how your interpretation of her performance might change, for example, if you knew that a score of 80 was the highest score on the arithmetic test, while 150 was the highest score in reading. Assume, further, that you had the additional information provided below:

Arithmetic and Reading Test Scores

	Arithmetic Score	*Reading Score*
Number of Items Correct (Raw Score)	80	80
Number of Students Taking Test	250	360
Number of Students Scoring Below 80	200	90

As you can see from the information provided, even though the raw scores were the same in reading and arithmetic, it would be incorrect to assume that Allison was performing at the same relative level in both areas. Although the raw scores were the same, she did better than a much higher proportion of the other youngsters on the arithmetic test than on the reading test. In reading, she did better than only 90 of the 360 children taking the test, while in arithmetic she did better than 200 of the 250 children taking the test. Thus, Allison did better than 80% of the other children in arithmetic but better than only 25% in reading.

The percentage of youngsters who fall below a particular score is referred to as the percentile rank of that score. The percentile rank is one of several types of norm-referenced scores that tell you how a child compared to other children. Grade and age scores, for example, tell you how a child compared to other youngsters of the same age or in the same grade, and standard scores tell you how close a child's score was to the average score on the test. All of these scores tell you a child's relative standing within a particular group.

Relative Performance versus Mastery

Why are we interested in relative standing? What does a child's relative standing on different tests tell you about his or her performance? Consider, again, the arithmetic and reading tests referred to above. As you can see, a norm-referenced score such as the percentile rank doesn't tell you very much about the skills a child has mastered in reading and arithmetic. On the other hand, knowing a child's relative standing in different subject areas does give you an idea of the child's relative strengths and weaknesses in ways that raw scores, and even criterion-referenced scores, cannot. The same raw score can be relatively high in one subject but at the bottom in another. It isn't until you know how the other children did that you have a point of reference to use in your evaluation. Unlike a criterion-referenced score, where a child's performance is compared to a criterion of mastery, with norm-referenced scores, a child's score is compared to the performance of other children.

Although many parents and educators feel uneasy about comparing youngsters, norm-referenced scores provide an important balance against criterion-referenced scores. As previously discussed, the criterion for mastery on many tests is set in quite an arbitrary fashion and, furthermore, tests in different areas often differ in difficulty. Consider, for example, the high school student who has an 87 average in a physics course after having grades of 97 and 98 in biology and chemistry. Is the student falling down in physics? Is the student's strength in biology and chemistry? Or is it that the physics tests are harder? One way of shedding light on the subject is to look at the student's relative standing in physics as compared to chemistry and biology. If the student was in the top 5% of the class in biology and chemistry, but did better than only 75% of the students in physics, then you would know that the student had shown more strength in biology and chemistry. If, on the other hand, the student was still in the top 5% of the physics class, even with an average of 87, then you would know that the student was relatively as strong in physics as in chemistry and biology. It is the comparison with the performance of others that enables you to put the student's performance into perspective. It is the assessment of a child's relative performance in different subjects that gives you a picture of the child's areas of strength and weakness.

As a matter of fact, an analysis of the typical performance of a group of youngsters is often used as the basis for determining the criterion of mastery. Consider, for example, how an athlete would qualify for the Olympics. Or, for that matter, how you would determine whether a preschooler displayed normal language development. In both cases you would be looking for the presence of certain skills. But the level of skill that would qualify an athlete for the Olympics, or enable you to classify a child's development as normal, would be determined by looking at the performance of others. The athlete's performance would be compared to the performance of other Olympic hopefuls, and the preschooler's performance would be compared to the typical performance of other preschoolers. In both cases, we would be interested in the individual's relative performance in comparison to a specified reference group.

As you can see, then, a norm-referenced score doesn't tell you what skills a child has mastered but rather how the child's performance on the skills being tested compares to the performance of others. Thus, if very few of the children mastered the skills that were tested, a child could receive a very high relative score with very little mastery of the material. Consider, for example, the spelling scores described below.

Spelling Scores of Five Third-Graders on a 50-Word Test

Student	Number of Words Correct
Adam	29
Beth	28
Craig	21
David	18
Emma	12

As you can see, none of the children in the above example had anywhere near all of the words correct. Nevertheless, if this were a norm-referenced test and this group was similar in performance to the norm group, Adam and Beth would have very high norm-referenced scores. These high scores would certainly not mean that they had demonstrated a high degree of mastery of the spelling words that were tested, but simply that they had mastered those words to a higher degree than the other children to whom they were being compared.

The Norm Group

In that norm-referenced scores are telling you how a child compared to a particular group of youngsters, it is very important to know the group with which the youngster is being compared. If, for example, you knew that a child fell at the 88th percentile on a test, you would know that the child did better than 88% of the youngsters with whom he or she was being compared. The meaning of that score could differ, however, depending upon the composition of the comparison group.

Assume, for example, that you have a seventh-grader who received a percentile rank of 88 on a test of arithmetic computation. Assuming that the comparison group was all other seventh-graders in the state, the score would be telling you that, statewide, your child did better than 88% of the other children in the same grade. That same percentile rank of 88 would have a very different meaning, however, if the comparison group, rather than being limited to seventh-graders, was composed of all children enrolled in junior high school. In the second instance, the comparison group would include children in grades seven through nine, and the percentile rank of 88 would mean that your child did better than 88% of all junior high school students in the state. Certainly, a percentile rank of 88 compared to all junior high school students represents a higher level of achievement than a percentile rank of 88 compared to only seventh graders. As you can see, then, a true understanding of the meaning of a norm-referenced score is not possible without information about the group to which the child is being compared.

In technical language, the comparison group is called the norm group, and the scores of the norm group are referred to as norms. Thus, norm-referenced scores tell you how a child compared to a particular norm group. It must be emphasized, however, that norms simply represent the performance of a particular group of students and in no way represent the mastery of a particular set of skills. If a child falls at the norm, it simply means that the child is performing at the same level as the average child in the norm group. There may be essential skills that the entire norm group didn't master, and performing at the norm does not mean that the child has learned what was expected.

On most standardized tests, the norm group will be a cross-section of youngsters in different grades selected from various parts of the country. When such is the case, the test is said to have national norms, and a child's score indicates how the child's performance compared to that of the youngsters in that national norm group.

On most of the more widely used tests, separate norms will be provided for each grade, and sometimes separate norms will also be provided for boys and girls and, on the secondary level, for students in different types of programs. Separate norms may be provided, for example, for students in vocational, commercial, and academic programs. Thus, if you have a child in an academic program who is preparing for college, the norms for academic students will tell you how that child compares to other students who are also preparing for college.

Sometimes, particularly in school districts where the youngsters generally score much higher or lower than average, local norms are also developed. In this case, the norm group will consist of youngsters from your area. Local norms are sometimes developed within one school district but may also be developed for a group of similar school districts, for all the schools in a particular city or group of cities, or for the schools in a particular region.

The importance of knowing the norm group to which a child is being compared can be seen in the following example. Assume that Andrew is in a school district in which performance is generally above the national average and that he received a percentile rank of 88 on a test of arithmetic computation when using national norms. Were local norms to be used, however, the same level of performance on the same test could yield a percentile rank of 53. What does this difference mean? How can the same raw score have two different percentile ranks? And which percentile rank is more accurate?

The difference occurs because, when local norms are used, Andrew is being compared to a relatively elite group. Compared to that group, a group composed of students who have had the advantage of superior educational benefits, his relative standing was lower than it was in the population at large.

Now consider Martina, a ninth-grader who is ranked relatively low on her high school's cross-country team. Although she may be an excellent runner, it is difficult to be ranked very high when your teammates include youngsters in the tenth, eleventh, and twelfth grades who are older, more physically mature, and more experienced. Compared to her teammates, a six-minute mile may put her at the 40th percentile. When she runs in a special race that is limited to ninth-graders, however, the same six-minute mile may put her at the 90th percentile. Has she run any better in the ninth-grade race? No, her time is the same as when she ran with her team. The difference is not in her performance, but in the group to which she is being compared.

The situation is the same when we compare performance based on national norms to performance based on local norms. Since norm-referenced scores are measures of relative performance, the norm-referenced score will vary depending on the group to which the child is being compared. When the child is being compared to other children in a superior school district, the percentile rank will be lower than when the child is compared to the general population of children in all types of districts. Neither score is more accurate or better. They simply provide you with different information that is useful in different situations.

National norms are useful for telling you how a child compares to other youngsters in the same grade across the country. They give you an indication of where the child stands on the basic skills that are taught in most schools in the country, but they are often not very useful for local decision making. Local norms, on the other hand, can be used for discriminating within the district among youngsters at different levels of performance. Local norms tell you how a child compares to other children within the same area and/or with the same educational opportunities.

It should be noted, of course, that a child won't always have a different score on local and national norms. In an average school district, the scores may be very similar. And when there is a difference, the child's score won't always be lower on the local norms. In a high-achieving school district, as illustrated above, the percentile rank will be higher on the national norms than on the local norms, while the reverse will be true for a low-achieving district.

Consider, for example, a school in a poor rural school district where the students generally score below average on the national norms. A top student in such a district may score at the 80th percentile on national norms, but the 95th percentile on local norms. In this case, the higher scoring group would be the national sample, and the child would do relatively better compared to the students in the local school district than when compared to a national sample of students.

It is also important to note that most norm-referenced tests are not re-normed every year. That is, once the scores for a particular norm group have been established, those same scores from the same norm group are used for several years. When you have a child's percentile rank on a test, then, that score does not necessarily tell you how the child ranked in comparison to other children who took the test at the same time. The score simply tells you how the child ranked in comparison to the particular norming group that was used in developing the norm-referenced scores. Thus, the child may be being compared to children who took the test many years ago and the score may be misleading.

We might not expect that there would be much change in the level of performance over a period of years, but consider the introduction of new instructional techniques and/or environmental variables such as television. Prior to the development of Sesame Street, for example, many youngsters had much less exposure to readiness tasks than they do today. Comparing the reading readiness performance of youngsters exposed to Sesame Street to a norm group who took the test prior to its development would most likely result in much higher scores for the later group. Thus, a youngster taking the test at the later date could obtain a relatively high score compared to the norm group that took the test in the past even though that youngster may be performing relatively poorly compared to others taking the test at the later time.

As you can see then, norm-referenced scores do not tell you what skills a child has mastered but rather how the child compares to a particular group of youngsters. In interpreting norm-referenced scores, it is important to know the norm group. Is the child being compared to other youngsters in the same grade? Is the norm group composed of youngsters with the same educational background? The answers to these questions are essential in order to fully understand the meaning of the score.

In the next chapter we will go into more detail concerning the different types of norm-referenced scores. It should be noted, however, that all norm-referenced scores, whether they are age or grade scores, percentile ranks, or standard scores, are scores that tell you how a child's performance on a test compared to the performance of a specified comparison group.

Chapter 9

Norms: Measures of Relative Performance

Let's say that Beth received a score of 43 on a county-wide spelling test. What would that score tell you? Did she do well? Or poorly? You really can't tell without some further information. You might want to know how many items there were on the test. After all, a score of 43 would have quite a different meaning if there were only 50 words on the test than if there were 100. You might also want to know how other children did. Even with 100 words on the test, a score of 43 might not be so bad if they were very difficult words and no one else had more than 30 words correct. On the other hand, if 90% of the children taking the test had over 50 words correct, Beth's score of 43 would have a very different meaning.

As you can see, the raw score, or number of items correct, does not provide enough information to evaluate a student's performance on the test. It is for that reason that raw scores are usually transformed into other types of scores. On classroom tests, for example, scores are often reported as percentages. Percentages indicate what percent of the items were answered correctly and are somewhat more useful than raw scores; they tell you the proportion of items answered correctly regardless of the number of items on the test and thereby enable you to compare performance on tests of different length.

If, for example, a child had 37 items correct on a 50-item arithmetic test one week, 28 items correct on a 35-item test the following week, and 60 items correct on a 75-item test the third week, it would be hard to tell on which of the tests the child did best. If, instead, you were told that the child had 74% of the problems correct on the first test and 80% on the second and third tests, you would immediately realize that the child correctly answered a greater proportion of the items on the later two tests than on the first. A higher proportion of items correct, however, does not necessarily mean a higher level of relative performance. On a difficult test, 74% may be the highest score in the class. On an easy test, almost all of the children may get more than 74% of the items correct. The percentage correct, then, doesn't tell us how a child performed relative to other children. In order to assess relative performance, we must look at norm-referenced scores.

Norm-referenced scores indicate how an individual child or a group of children compares to a larger comparison group. These scores may take a variety of forms: grade or age equivalent scores, percentile ranks, or standard scores. Each of these scores is a measure of relative performance, a measure that indicates how a child performed relative to a specific group of children called a norm group. Each type of norm-referenced score, however, provides somewhat different information about a child's performance.

GRADE-EQUIVALENT SCORES

Grade norms, or grade-equivalent scores, are widely reported for the achievement and aptitude tests administered in the schools. These scores indicate the grade level that is deemed equivalent to a particular level of performance on a test. A grade-equivalent score of 6.5, for example, would be interpreted as a level of performance that is equivalent to the typical performance of youngsters in the fifth month of sixth grade. Note that the number before the decimal represents the grade and that the number following the decimal represents the month of the school year. A grade equivalent score of 4.10 therefore would represent the tenth month of fourth grade, and a score of 11.3 would represent the third month of eleventh grade.

At first glance, these scores seem to be easily interpretable and meaningful. In fact, however, these scores are less precise than they seem and they can be misleading. Particularly at the secondary school level, there are serious questions as to their use. In order to understand why they are so troublesome, let us first look at how they are developed.

The Development of Grade-Equivalent Scores

When you see a score of 6.3, for example, and interpret it to mean performance typical of the third month of sixth grade, you assume that someone has actually determined how the typical child in the third month of sixth grade performs. In fact, however, grade-equivalent scores are not based on actual performance at each month within a grade. Instead, a large sample of students at selected grade levels is tested at one time during the school year. Third graders, for example, may be tested in April, and fourth graders in May. Sixth graders may be tested in October, while fifth graders may take the test in November.

Although grade norms appear to represent typical performance at every month of every grade, what actually happens, however, is that hypothetical performance levels are derived by interpolation. That is, grade-equivalent scores for points at which no testing occurred are estimated from the scores obtained by the groups tested at selected points in the school year.

Consider, for example, the data in Figure 9.1, which represent the average test performance of four hypothetical norm groups in grades three through six. Each box on the graph represents the average score of youngsters in a particular grade tested at a particular month during the school year. As you can see, there is only one box for each grade. Third-graders were tested in April, and the box representing their average performance—15 items correct—was placed on the graph above the point representing the eighth month (April) of third grade. Similarly, since sixth-graders were tested in January, the box plotted for sixth-graders was placed above the fifth month (January) of sixth grade. The boxes are connected with straight lines, assuming steady growth from grade to grade. Additionally, the lines are extended for grades below the third and above the sixth.

Now consider a student who attains a score of 20. The grade equivalent score may be obtained by first finding the point where the score of 20 falls on the vertical axis. We then draw a line from that point across to where it intersects the line of the graph (the horizontal dotted line). A second line (the vertical dotted line) is then drawn from the point where the first line intersects the graph line to the horizontal axis. The grade equivalent score is 4.2, which corresponds to the point where the vertical dotted line crosses the axis showing the grade-equivalent scores.

In fact, however, no children were tested in the second month of fourth grade, and we do not know how the typical child in the second month of

Figure 9.1
Grade-Equivalent Scores Derived from Four Actual Scores

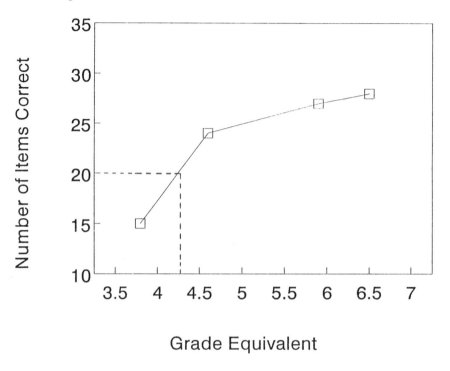

fourth grade would actually perform on the test. When we say therefore that a student has a grade-equivalent score of 4.2, we really don't know if the child is performing at the same level as the typical child in the second month of fourth grade. These scores are estimates of what would be expected at a particular grade level and do not take into account the fluctuations in performance that naturally occur in students' progress over the course of the school year.

The process described above is referred to as interpolation, and the estimated grade equivalent scores are interpolated scores. They reflect estimated performance rather than actual performance. The interpolated scores assume that there is even, "straight line" growth from one point to another. It is assumed, in other words, that growth over the school year is smooth, without spurts and declines. In fact, however, we know that such is not the case. Growth does not progress evenly, and there are different rates of growth at different times in the school year and at different levels of schooling. Students tested right after summer vacation, for example, may do worse in mathematics than they did on the same test the previous spring. Or excitement about the upcoming holidays may depress performance in the days just before Thanksgiving.

Furthermore, the rate of growth in basic skills is much greater in the early grades than it is later on. Consequently, a month of growth in first grade is very different from a month of growth in twelfth grade. In interpreting grade-equivalent scores, a difference of six months at first grade can mean a significant difference in achievement, while a difference of six months at eleventh grade may represent negligible growth.

Consider the typical beginning first grader and a child who is reading at a third-grade level. The difference in reading ability between the beginning first-grader and the typical third-grader is so great that you really don't need a test to determine that there's a major difference in their reading skills. Now, however, consider the difference between a typical tenth grader and a typical twelfth grader. Although there is the same two-year difference between first and third grade as there is between tenth and twelfth grade, the growth over the two-year period from tenth to twelfth grade is much less than in the lower grades and, at the high school level, the difference in ability would be much harder to detect.

In the high school grades, as a matter of fact, it is very hard even to determine what a grade-equivalent means. When students are studying subjects such as trigonometry, algebra, and geometry, what they know at each grade level is a function of the courses to which they were exposed. Knowing the difference between the sine and the cosine, or understanding how to solve simultaneous equations, is not necessarily a function of a student's grade but of which particular courses in math a student has taken. At this level, grade-equivalent scores really lose their meaning, and they are inappropriate for use in reporting scores.

Testing companies may use mathematical formulas rather than a graph to estimate the grade equivalents of different scores, and statistical techniques are often used to equate different levels of a test so that students in different grades are not necessarily taking the same examination. Nevertheless, the premise is the same, and the various procedures used present all of the limitations described above. These same limitations apply to age norms or age-equivalent scores. Although age norms are not as commonly used as grade norms, they are still reported for some types of assessments. They are developed in very much the same way as are grade norms except that the norm groups represent children of different ages rather than in different grades. Regardless of whether age or grade norms are reported, however, the same limitations apply.

What Do Grade-Equivalent Scores Tell You?

Given the problems described above, you can begin to see that, although grade-equivalent scores may look easy to interpret, they are really not what they appear to be. Let's consider, then, what these scores do tell you about test performance and what they don't.

At any grade level, grade-equivalent scores indicate whether a child's performance on a particular test is at about the same level as others in the same grade, below others in the grade, or above others in the grade. The comparison, however, is not necessarily with others in the child's school or school district but with the students in the norm group.

Assume, for example, that the following grade-equivalent scores were attained by Carlos at the beginning of third grade on the reading and mathematics portions of an achievement test battery:

Area Tested	Grade-Equivalent Score
Total Mathematics	4.2
Computation	3.8
Applications	4.4
Reasoning	4.1
Total Reading	6.5
Comprehension	6.7
Vocabulary	6.4

Looking at these scores, you can certainly say that he is doing somewhat better than the typical third-grader in the norm group. At first glance, however, you might also think that he did better in reading than in math. After all, his math scores are only about one year above grade level, while his reading scores are three years above grade level. Although it might seem logical to draw this conclusion, the scores do not provide you with a basis for these conclusions. In fact, all you can say is that Carlos scored above grade level in both reading and mathematics.

Why can't you say more than this? You can't make comparisons between the performance in reading and math because, with grade-equivalent scores, we do not know whether a month of growth in one subject is equivalent to a month of growth in another. We do not necessarily have equal units of growth in different subjects. It may well be, for example, that the percentage of third graders with reading grade scores above 6.5 is higher than the percentage with grade scores above 4.2 in math. In other words, even though

Carlos's grade score is higher in reading than in math, his percentile rank may be higher in math than in reading. In fact, this often is the case. Good readers may be able to perform quite well on reading tasks that are beyond what is typical for their grade. It is unlikely, however, that youngsters will be able to perform mathematical operations that they have not been taught in school. Even though a child may be very good in math, it is unlikely for the child to be able to do problems dealing with fractions or percentages or decimals before being taught these topics in school.

It is also inappropriate to make comparisons about differences in grade scores at different grade levels. Assume, for example, that Allison had a grade equivalent score in reading of 6.5 in third grade and 12.5 in ninth grade. Although in each case she scored three years above grade level, these three years do not have the same meaning at third grade and at sixth. Given the fact that so much growth occurs in the elementary school years and that reading skill tends to level out in the upper grades, the three-year difference at third grade represents a much more significant difference than it does in high school. Although her performance is above average in both cases, the three-year difference at third grade represents more of a difference than it does at ninth grade.

A further problem with grade equivalent scores is that it is sometimes assumed that a child could or should be doing work at the level equivalent to the grade score attained on a test. Parents may ask, for example, why their third-grader, who had a grade equivalent score of 6.10 in math, isn't doing sixth grade mathematics. Typically, however, the third grader who attains a grade equivalent score of 6.10 usually does not have the same pattern of response as the typical sixth-grader with the same score. They may both get the same number of items correct, but the third grader will usually obtain this score by very rapidly and accurately answering the types of problems that have been learned by third grade. The third-grader will do very well on the simple addition, subtraction, and multiplication problems, for example, but won't be able to do the problems requiring long division, decimals, and fractions. The typical sixth-grader, on the other hand, is usually less accurate—and may make more errors on the less advanced work than will the third-grader—but will be able to correctly answer the problems requiring the more advanced mathematical skills that the third-grader hasn't learned. In other words, the grade-equivalent score of 6.10 indicates that the third-grader is exceptionally proficient at what he or she has learned, not that sixth-grade skills have been attained. The sixth-grader, on the other hand, has learned more but hasn't mastered that material quite as thoroughly as the third-grader has mastered what was learned in the earlier grades.

It should also be noted that, as with any norms, grade norms should not be taken as standards that all children should be expected to meet. Grade-equivalent scores are based on the average score in the norm group and, by definition, 50% of the children in the norm group must fall at or below the group average. In a class of children comparable to those in the norm group, then, 50% of the class may also be expected to score at or below the norm. Even though the average performance of a typical class might be expected to fall at the norm, we would expect about half the children in the class to score above the norm and about half to score below.

As you can see, then, grade scores are not really what they seem to be. They give an indication of whether or not a child is performing at or near grade level compared to a particular norm group. Nevertheless, grade-equivalent scores are still very commonly reported, and you should know what they do and do not tell you. Because of the many limitations of grade norms, percentile norms are usually preferred.

PERCENTILE NORMS

When percentile norms are used, a child's score will usually be reported as a percentile rank. The percentile rank tells you what percentage of the students in the norm group had scores that were lower than that of the child in question. If a child received a percentile rank of 80 on a test, for example, that child's test score was higher than that of 80% of the youngsters in the norm group. If the child received a percentile rank of 98, the score was better than that of 98% of the youngsters in the group; if the child received a percentile rank of 20, the child's score was higher than that of 20% of the youngsters in the norm group.

Sometimes, rather than reporting the score as a percentile rank, you will simply be told that a child's score fell at the 80th percentile, or at the 99th percentile. Any percentile is simply the score below which fell a specified percentage of the scores within a group. The 80th percentile is the score below which 80% of the scores fell, and the 99th percentile is the score below which 99% of the scores fall. If a child's score is at the 80th percentile, then, it means that 80% of the scores fell below that child's score.

Percentile norms do not tell you the percentage of items that were correctly answered. If 98% of the norm group correctly answered only 5% of the items, then a child correctly answering 6% of the items would have a percentile rank of 99. On the other hand, if 98% of the children in the norm group correctly answered 95% of the test items, then a child correctly answering 90% of the items might have a percentile rank as low as 1 or 2.

In other words, it is possible to have a very high percentile rank while answering many of the test items incorrectly and to have a very low percentile rank while answering most of them correctly.

Referring to Table 9.1, we can see that the reading test was easier than the arithmetic test. That is, more children had high scores on the reading test than on the arithmetic test. Consequently, a student who had 16 out of 20 items (or 80% of the items) correct on the arithmetic test had a percentile rank of 90, while a student with 16 out of 20 items correct on the reading test had a percentile rank of only 50. The same percentage of items correct thus corresponded to a higher percentile rank on the arithmetic test than on the reading test. As you can see, then, the percentile rank indicates how a child compared to other children, not how many items were answered correctly.

As with any type of norms, the percentile rank of a score will differ in reference to different norm groups. A score of 80 on a high school English test may put a child at the 85th percentile when compared to vocational students, but at the 60th percentile as compared to college-bound seniors. The college-bound seniors are a higher achieving group than the vocational students; thus, a score that exceeds the scores of 85% of vocational students is higher than the scores of only 60% of the college-bound seniors. Similarly, a score of 30 on a reading readiness test could put a child at the 75th

Table 9.1

Percentile Rank Equivalents to Scores on a Reading and an Arithmetic Test

Number of Items Correct	Percentile Rank on the Reading test	Percentile Rank on the Arithmetic Test
20	99	99
19	90	99
18	80	98
17	65	95
16	50	90
15	40	84
14	30	78
13	22	70
12	17	62
11	10	54
10	5	46
9	1	40
8	-	32
7	-	25
6	-	15
3	-	8
2	-	2
1	-	1

percentile compared to a national sample of first-graders but at the 50th percentile compared to the first-graders in a well-to-do suburban district. In order to understand the significance of a percentile rank, then, you must know the norm group that is being used for comparison.

In interpreting percentile norms, it is also important to realize that equal differences in percentile ranks do not necessarily correspond to equal differences in performance. One might assume, for example, that the difference in performance between the child who performs at the 45th percentile and the child who performs at the 60th percentile is the same as the difference between the child who performs at the 80th percentile and the child who performs at the 95th percentile. After all, there are 15 percentile ranks between the 45th and 60th percentiles, and there are also 15 percentile ranks between the 80th and 95th percentiles. Unfortunately, however, this assumption is incorrect.

To illustrate this point, let's refer to the reading scores in Table 9.1. A score of 19 is equivalent to a percentile rank of 90, while a score of 18 is equivalent to a percentile rank of 80. In this instance, a 1-point difference in the number of items correct corresponds to a 10-point difference in percentile ranks. At the same time, however, although a score of 18 items correct is equivalent to a percentile rank of 80, a score of 17 items correct is equivalent to percentile rank of only 65. In this second instance, the same 1-point difference in the number of items correct corresponds to a 15-point difference in percentile ranks.

Why is it that in one case a 1-point difference in the raw score results in a 10-point difference in raw scores while, in another case, the same 1-point difference in raw scores results in a 15-point difference in percentile ranks? It is because the difference in percentile ranks reflects the percentage of people who fell between the two scores. The fact that the difference in percentile ranks between a raw score of 18 and a raw score of 19 was 10 percentile ranks means that 10% of the students fell between those two scores. If 30% of the students fell between those scores, then there would have been a 30-point difference in percentile ranks, and if 60 percent of the students fell between those two scores, then there would have been a 60-point difference in percentile ranks. As you can see, then, the difference in percentile ranks is not a function of the difference in score points but simply the number of students who fell between those two scores. In some cases, a difference of ten items correct on a test can correspond to a difference of two percentile ranks, while in other cases the same difference of ten items correct can correspond to an 80-point difference in percentile ranks.

This problem occurs whenever we have percentile ranks; equivalent differences in percentile ranks do not necessarily correspond to equivalent differences in test performance. It is for this reason that standard scores are preferable.

STANDARD SCORE NORMS

Standard score norms include a variety of different types of scores. Scores such as z-scores, T-scores, IQ scores, *SAT* scores, stanines, and NCE scores are standard scores. The advantage of these scores over percentile norms is that equal differences between standard scores correspond to equal differences in test performance.

Standard scores are scores that are based on a statistic called the standard deviation. The standard deviation is a measure that estimates the degree to which the scores in a group differ from their average. Assume, for example, that Amy and Beth received the following quiz scores in French:

Amy	Beth
84	87
84	86
84	85
84	84
84	83
84	82
84	81

If we find the average of Amy's test scores, which is referred to as the mean, it would be equal to 84. Since all of her scores are exactly the same, they are all exactly equal to the average; there is zero difference between each of the scores and the average. The standard deviation, which tells us the average difference between each of the scores and the average score, would thus be equal to zero. Beth's scores, on the other hand, are not all the same. Beth's average is also 84, but the standard deviation of her scores is equal to 2. In this case, the scores are not all the same and are not all equal to the average. The standard deviation tells us that, on average, the scores differ from the average by about 2 points. If the standard deviation is small, it means that the scores are close together. The greater the difference between each of the scores and their average, the larger the standard deviation will be.

Standard scores tell us how many standard deviations away from the average of the norm group a particular student scored. Assume, for example, that we had an arithmetic test on which the class average was 80 and the standard deviation was 2. A student who had a score of 82 would be one standard deviation above the average, and a student with a score of 84 would be two standard deviations above the average. Similarly, a student with a score of 78 would be one standard deviation below the average. In contrast to percentile ranks, standard scores are not based on the number or the percentage of students that fell below a particular score, but on the distance between that score and the average as measured in standard deviation units.

The *z*-Score

The basic standard score, the *z*-score, simply indicates the number of standard deviations above or below the average a particular score fell. If the *z*-score is 0, the score is equal to the average. If the *z*-score is +2, the score is two standard deviations above the average; if the *z*-score is −1.5, the score is one and a half standard deviations below the average.

Assume, for example, that we had a test on which the average was 100 and the standard deviation was equal to 15. If Martina had a score of 85 on the test, her *z*-score would be −1 because her score was one standard deviation—15 points—below the average. If Alice had a score of 100, which was equal to the average, her *z*-score would be 0; her score was zero standard deviations away from the average. Similarly, if Elena had a score of 115, her *z*-score would be +1 because her score was one standard deviation of 15 points above the average.

As you can see, a *z*-score may be positive or negative; a positive *z*-score indicates that the score is above the average, and a negative *z*-score indicates that the score is below the average. It is thus very important to retain the sign of the *z*-score; a *z*-score of +1 is quite different from a *z*-score of −1.

You may also note that the distance between the *z*-scores is proportional to the distance between the raw scores. For each 15-point difference between score points on the test, there will be a 1-point difference in *z*-scores. We know therefore that the difference between a *z*-score of −1 and a *z*-score of 0 reflects the same 15-point difference in score points as does the 1-point difference between a *z*-score of 0 and a *z*-score of +1. Furthermore, any 2-point difference in *z*-scores will reflect a 30-point difference in score points, and any .5-point difference in *z*-scores will reflect a 7.5-point difference in score points. Unlike percentile ranks, equal differences in *z*-scores always reflect equal differences in score points.

The *z*-scores may also be used to compare performance on different tests and in different subjects. Consider, for example, the math and English tests described below. Note that the average score is referred to as the mean.

Mean and Standard Deviation on a Math and an English Test

Math	*English*
Mean = 76	Mean = 84
SD = 3	SD = 4

If a student received scores of 82 on both tests, our first impression might be that the student did equally well in both subjects. If we look at the test statistics, however, we can see that not only were the scores on the math test lower than those on the English test, but that the students were grouped more closely around the average on the math test. A score of 82 in math, then, has quite a different meaning from a score of 82 in English. If we were to use *z*-scores rather than the raw scores for making our comparison, this difference would be apparent.

In math, a score of 82 would be two standard deviations above the average and would be equivalent to a *z*-score of +2. In English, however, a score of 82 would be a half standard deviation below the average and would be equivalent to a *z*-score of −.5. Even though the raw scores are exactly the same, the *z*-scores indicate that a score of 82 reflects relatively better performance in math, where the score is above average, than it does in English, where the score is below average. The *z*-score, then, enables you to compare the relative performance on two separate tests. It should be noted, however, that such comparisons assume equivalent norm groups on both tests.

z-Scores and the Normal Curve

If you graphed the scores of the norm group on most of the standardized tests administered in the schools, the graph would form a bell-shaped curve as illustrated in Figure 9.2. This curve is referred to as a normal distribution. The height of the curve at any point represents the number of students whose scores fell at that point in the distribution; the highest point on the curve is at the mean (average) score, and the height of the curve decreases as the distance from the mean increases. The shape of the normal curve reflects the fact that most students are grouped around the average; as you move away from the average toward extremely high or extremely low scores, you find fewer and fewer students.

Figure 9.2
Relationship among Different Standard Scores and Percentile Ranks in a Normal Distribution

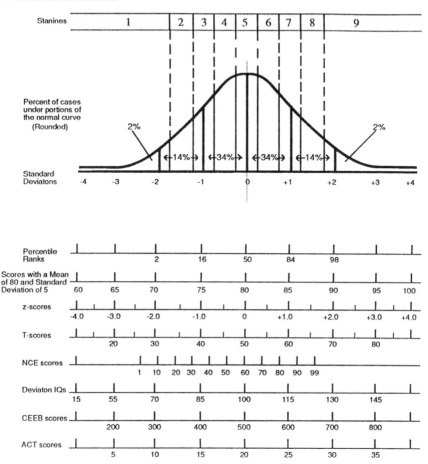

There is a mathematical formula for the normal distribution that enables us to determine exactly how many scores fall at each point along the curve. It is not necessary, however, to understand the mathematics behind the normal curve to understand the implications of the distribution for interpreting scores. It is sufficient to be aware that, whenever we have a normal distribution, a specified percentage of scores will fall between the average score and each z-score value. As illustrated in Figure 9.2, approximately 34% of the students' scores will fall between the average and whatever score is equivalent to a z-score of +1, approximately 14% of the students' scores will fall between the score that is equivalent to a z-score of +1 and the score that is equivalent to a *z*-score of +2, and about 2% of the scores will be above the score that is equivalent to a *z*-score of +2. Since the curve is symmetrical, another 34% of the students' scores will fall between the average and a *z*-score of –1, another 14% of the students' scores will fall between the scores that are equivalent to *z*-scores of –1 and –2, and another 2% will be below the score that is equivalent to a *z*-score of –2.

If we have a normal distribution of scores and we know a student's *z*-score, the above information will enable us to determine the student's percentile rank. It is important to note, however, that the relationship between *z*-scores and percentile ranks is based on the assumption that the scores are normally distributed.

z-Scores and Percentile Ranks

To illustrate the relationship between *z*-scores and percentile ranks, let's assume that Russell has a score of 85 on a math test with a normal distribution of scores. If the average on the test is equal to 80 and the standard deviation is equal to 5, Russell's *z*-score would be equal to +1. Since we know that 34% of the scores in any normal distribution fall between the average score and a *z*-score of +1, we know that Russell did better than the 34% of the students with scores between 80 and 85. He also did better than the 50% of the students who fell below the average. Adding together the 50% of the students who fell below the average and the 34% who fell between the average and the score of 85, we can see that Russell did better than 84% of the students. In other words, Russell had a percentile rank of 84.

Similarly, if Melissa had a score of 75, which is equivalent to a *z*-score of –1, she would have done better than the 2% of the students who fell below a *z*-score of –2 as well as the 14% of the students who fell between the *z*-scores of –1 and –2. Melissa would have had a percentile rank of 16. We could similarly find the percentile ranks of the students who had *z*-scores of –2, 0, and +2. The conversion from *z*- scores to percentile ranks is not limited to these particular *z*-scores, however; there are tables that enable us to find the percentile rank equivalent to any *z*-score. We could find the percentile rank equivalent of a *z*-score of +2.3 as well as of a *z*-score of –1.6.

Although the scores on most classroom tests do not form a normal distribution, most of the commonly used standardized tests are constructed in such a way that the scores are distributed normally. Such conversions can be particularly useful, then, when we want to make comparisons among tests for which different types of scores are reported. Even though the scores on one test are reported as percentile ranks and the scores on another are reported as standard scores, a student's relative performance on the two tests can be compared. If a student had a percentile rank of 86 on one test, for example, and a z-score of +2 on another, we know that he did relatively better on the test on which his z-score is +2.

Although we can convert z-scores to percentile ranks when we have a normal distribution, it is important to remember the difference between them: equal differences in z-scores reflect equal differences in score points on the test, while equal differences in percentile ranks do not. This distinction is illustrated by the data in Table 9.2.

As may be noted, the difference in raw score (that is, the number of test items correct) between each successive student included in Table 9.2 was 5 points; Carlos's score was 5 points higher than Donna's, Ben's was 5 points higher than Carlos's, and Alicia's was 5 points higher than Ben's. Although Carlos and Donna differed on the test by only 5 points, this 5-point difference on the test corresponded to a difference of 34 percentile ranks. The 5-point difference on the test resulted in a 34-point difference in percentile ranks because 34% of the students fell between Donna and Carlos: Donna's score was at the average and Carlos's score was one standard deviation above the average and, in a normal distribution of scores, 34% of the students fall between the average and the score that is one standard deviation above the average.

Now look at Ben. Ben also differed from Carlos by only 5 points on the test. Since only 14 percent of the students fell between scores of 85 and 90, however, Ben's percentile rank is only 14 points higher than Carlos's. In this case, a 5-point difference in score points on the test resulted in a difference of only 14 percentile ranks. If you now look at Alicia's score,

Table 9.2
Students' Raw Scores, Percentile Ranks, and z-Scores in a Normal Distribution of Test Scores with a Mean of 80 and a Standard Deviation of 5

Student	Raw Score	Diff.	%ile Rank	Diff.	z-Score	Diff.
Alicia	95		99		+3	
	}	5	}	1	}	1
Ben	90		98		+2	
	}	5	}	14	}	1
Carlos	85		84		+1	
	}	5	}	34	}	1
Donna	80		50		0	

you can see that the 5-point difference between Alicia's raw score and Ben's raw score corresponded to only a 1-point difference in percentile ranks, reflecting that fact that only 1% of the students had scores between 90 and 95. As you can see, then, equal differences in score points do not always correspond to equal differences in percentile ranks.

Whenever we have a normal distribution, most of the students' scores are bunched together at the middle of the distribution, and a jump of a few score points may account for a relatively high percentage of the students. As you move toward the upper and lower ends of the distribution, however, the students are more spread out, and more score points have to be covered to account for the same percentage of students. Thus, at the middle of the distribution, a very small difference in score points may account for a large difference in percentile ranks, while at the upper and lower extremes of the distribution a large difference in actual test performance may account for a very small difference in percentile ranks.

Now, however, look at the z-scores that correspond to the raw scores of each of the students in Table 9.2. Every 5-point difference in score points corresponds to a 1-point difference in z-scores. In other words, the difference in z-scores is proportional to the difference in score points on the test. Where there is a 5-point difference in score points between Alicia and Ben, there is a 1-point difference in z-scores; the 5-point difference in score points between Ben and Carlos also corresponds to a 1-point difference in z-scores, as does the 5-point difference in score points between Carlos and Donna.

Furthermore, every 10-point difference in score points corresponds to a 2-point difference in z-scores. The 10-point difference in score points between Alicia and Carlos corresponds to a 2-point difference in z-scores (+3 minus +1), as does the 10-point difference between Donna and Ben. Similarly, the 15-point difference between Donna and Alicia corresponds to a 3-point difference in z-scores. As may be seen, the difference between two students' z-scores is proportional to the difference in their raw scores on the test.

Although we may convert z-scores to percentile ranks, however, these two types of norm-referenced scores cannot be interpreted in the same way. Equal differences in z-scores correspond to equal differences in test scores, but this relationship is lost when test scores are converted to percentile ranks. Equal differences in percentile ranks may not be assumed to correspond to equal differences in test performance.

Not all standard scores are reported as z-scores, however, and it is useful to be familiar with some of the other scores that are used. All of these scores have the same properties as z-scores; the different forms are chosen primarily for convenience. With the z-score, not only are fractional values common, but it is quite easy to make a clerical error that would confuse two scores. A z-score of +2 is quite different from a z-score of –2, but a simple clerical error involving the omission of the sign could eliminate this difference. To eliminate this problem as well as the fractional values that may occur with z-scores, other forms of standard scores are often used instead.

T-Scores, NCE Scores, IQ Scores, and Stanines

T-scores, NCE scores, IQ scores, and stanines are other commonly used forms of standard scores. All are transformations of the z-score and have the desirable properties of the z-score described above.

Let's first consider T-scores. With T-scores, the average (mean) score is assigned a value of 50. If a child's score is equal to the average score in the norm group, that child will be assigned a T-score of 50. As may be seen in Figure 9.2, a z-score of 0 is thus equal to a T-score of 50. As with z-scores, the difference between each score and the average is measured in standard deviations. With T-scores, however, each standard deviation is equivalent to 10 points on the scale of T-scores. If a child's score is one standard deviation above the average, then, that child will have a T-score that is equal to 60.

Assume, for example, that we have a set of normally distributed math scores with an average of 80 and a standard deviation of 5. If Russell has a score of 85, which is one standard deviation above the average (and equivalent to a z-score of +1), he will have a T-score of 60. His score will be 10 points above the average of the T-scores. Similarly if Melissa has a score of 75, which is one standard deviation below the average, she will have a T-score of 40. Her score will be 10 points below the average of the T-scores. As further illustrated in Figure 9.2, a child whose score is two standard deviations above the average will have a T-score of 70, and a child whose score is three standard deviations above the average will have a T-score of 80. Similarly, a child whose score is two standard deviations below the average will have a T-score of 30, and a child whose score is three standard deviations below the average will have T-score of 20. As with z-scores, T-score values may also fall between these values; a child whose score is one-half of a standard deviation above the average, for example, will have a T-score of 55.

Similarly, most IQ scores are standard scores, where the average score of a particular age group is assigned a value of 100 and the standard deviation is equal to 15 IQ points. Referring again to Figure 9.2, if Maria's score on an IQ test is two standard deviations above the average for her age group, you can see that her IQ score will be equal to 130. If Elizabeth's IQ score is at the average for her age group, she will have an IQ score of 100. A child with an IQ score of 145 would be three standard deviations above the average, and a child with an IQ of 85 would be one standard deviation below.

Another type of standard score that is frequently reported is the Normal Curve Equivalent, or NCE. NCEs are standard scores on which the average score is assigned a value of 50 and the standard deviation is assigned a value of 21.06. Although it may seem odd to assign a value of 21.06 to the standard deviation, this value was chosen so that the NCE scores will coincide with percentile ranks at the 1st, 50th, and 99th percentiles. NCE scores, however, may be interpreted in the same way as any other standard scores. A student whose score is one standard deviation above the average, for example, will have an NCE score of 71.06, which is equal to 50 + 21.06.

The scores on the *SAT* are also variations of the basic standard score. *SAT* scores are equivalent to standard scores with a mean of 500 and a standard deviation of 100. If a student's score is one standard deviation above the average of the norm group on the *SAT*, then, the student will have an *SAT* score of about 600. A student with an *SAT* score of 500 has performed at about the average of the norm group, and a student with a score of 800 has scored approximately three standard deviations above the average. *ACT* scores are standard scores with a mean of 20 and a standard deviation of 5. An *ACT* score of 25, then, is equivalent to an *SAT* score of 600.

Another type of standard score that is often reported is the stanine. Stanines are somewhat different from the other standard scores, however, in that a single stanine value is assigned to a band of scores. Each stanine is one-half of a standard deviation wide and there are nine stanines; "stanine," in fact, is a shortened form of "standard nine." Referring again to Figure 9.2, the stanines are represented by the alternately shaded areas under the normal curve. You can see that the middle stanine, which has a value of 5, extends from the point that is one-quarter of a standard deviation below the average to the point that is one-quarter of a standard deviation above the average. All scores falling within that stanine band are assigned a stanine score of 5. If, for example, Jessica had a score of 86 on an examination with an average of 85 and a standard deviation of 5, her score would fall within this band and she would have a stanine score of 5.

Referring again to Figure 9.2, you can see that the next highest stanine extends from the point that is one-quarter of a standard deviation above the average to the point that is three-quarters of a standard deviation above the average; this stanine band has a value of 6. The seventh stanine extends from three-quarters of a standard deviation above the average to one and one-quarter standard deviations above the average, and the eighth stanine extends from one and one-quarter standard deviations above the average to one and three-quarters standard deviations above the average. The ninth stanine then includes all scores that are more than one and three-quarters standard deviations above the average.

On the lower side, the fourth stanine extends from one-quarter of a standard deviation below the average to three-quarters of a standard deviation below the average; the third stanine extends form three-quarters of a standard deviation below the average to one and one-quarter standard deviations below the average; the second stanine extends from one and one-quarter standard deviations below the average to one and three-quarters standard deviations below the average; and the first stanine includes all scores that are more than one and three-quarters standard deviations below the average.

If Martina had a score of 90 on an examination with an average of 85 and a standard deviation of 5, her score would be one standard deviation above the average. Her score would fall into the seventh stanine and she would have a stanine score of 7. Douglas, with a score of 89, would fall into the same stanine and would also have a stanine score of 7. Richard, with a score of 75, is two standard deviations below the average and would fall into the lowest stanine; he would have a stanine score of 1, as would David with a score of 72. In interpreting stanine scores, it is customary to refer to stanine scores of 4, 5, and 6 as average, stanine scores of 1, 2, and 3 as below average, and stanine scores of 7, 8, and 9 as above average. Douglas and Martina then could be said to have performed above average on the test, while Richard and David performed below average.

The idea behind stanines is that small differences between scores may be due to measurement error rather than to real differences in ability. Thus, scores that are close together are assigned the same stanine score. Of course, scores that are close together but fall near the dividing score of the stanine may have different stanine scores. Nevertheless, stanines tend to de-emphasize differences among scores that may be due to error. Stanine scores are a form of standard score; with stanines, the mean score is assigned a stanine value of 5 and the standard deviation is assigned a value of 2. Thus, a score that is one standard deviation above the mean is equal to a stanine of 7; a score that is one and a half standard deviations above the mean is equal to a stanine of 8; and a score that is two standard deviations above the mean is equal to a stanine of 9. Similarly, a score that is one standard deviation below the mean is equal to a stanine of 3; a score that is one and a half standard deviations below the mean is equal to a stanine of 2; and a score that is two standard deviations below the mean is equal to a stanine of 1. The difference between stanines and other standard scores, however, is that there are only nine stanine values and scores within the half standard deviation bands illustrated in Figure 9.2 are all assigned the same stanine value.

Comparing Different Types of Scores

Students take a number of different tests, the scores on which are not all reported in the same way. On a scholastic aptitude test, for example, the reported score may be an IQ score or, perhaps, an *SAT* or *PSAT* score. On achievement tests, scores are likely to be reported as percentile ranks, stanines, NCEs, or T-scores.

Assume, for example, that Dennis received the following scores at the end of fifth grade:

IQ = 125

Reading Comprehension: NCE = 75

Arithmetic Computation: Percentile Rank = 70

Science Achievement: T = 60

Social Studies: Grade Score = 8.7

How would we compare his relative performance on these different tests? We would use the information described above and illustrated in Figure 9.2 regarding the relationships among these different norm-referenced scores.

We know, for example, that Dennis's IQ score of 125 is between one and two standard deviations above average, which puts him at somewhere between the 84th and 98th percentiles. His reading comprehension score is slightly more than one standard deviation above the mean of NCE scores, which puts him a little above the 84th percentile in this area. His arithmetic score, which is at the 70th percentile, is below his reading comprehension score; his science score, which is one standard deviation above the mean of T-scores, puts him at the 84th percentile in science. His social studies score indicates above-average performance for his grade in this area.

Even though Dennis's scores have been reported in a variety of different forms, we can see that he scored above average both on the scholastic aptitude test and on the various achievement tests with which he was tested. If we then look more closely at his relative performance in the different subject areas, we can see that he performed best in reading, with somewhat lower performance in science and in arithmetic. Although we know that his social studies score was above average, we cannot make a direct conversion between this grade-equivalent score and the scores in the other subjects. Knowing the relationship between standard scores and percentile ranks, then, we can make comparisons of a child's relative performance across a range of tests. It should be remembered, however, that these comparisons assume equivalent norm groups and normal score distributions.

In conclusion, measures of relative performance enable us to interpret the meaning of a child's test scores in reference to the performance of other children. A child who has a score of 80 in arithmetic, for example, is not necessarily doing well. If this performance corresponds to a percentile rank of 10, his performance is relatively poor. On the other hand, if his performance corresponds to a z-score of +2, we know that he is doing comparatively well.

It must be remembered, however, that a sound evaluation of a child's performance does not rest on the scores alone, but in our ability to use those scores intelligently. Measures of relative performance do not tell us whether Russell's teacher covered the work on the test or whether Beth was absent and had gaps in her preparation. The scores can provide some very useful information but, in order to be truly useful, their uses and limitations must be understood.

Chapter 10

Using Test Scores in Educational Decision Making

When test scores are used in making educational decisions, it is important not only to understand the meaning of the scores but also to evaluate the information they provide. Although it is certainly important to recognize that a percentile rank of 84 represents a higher degree of relative performance than does an NCE of 50, it is equally important to recognize that neither the NCE of 50 nor the percentile rank of 84 is necessarily indicative of a child's ability.

Let's assume, for example, that Jason, who has recently immigrated to the United States, received a percentile rank of 84 on a mathematics achievement test and an NCE of 50 on a science achievement test. If we consider the scores in isolation, we might conclude that Jason did relatively better in arithmetic than in science, that he has a relatively better grasp of mathematics than he does of science. When we take other factors into account, however, we might question this conclusion.

It may be that the science test was highly verbal and that the score reflected his limited command of the English language. Or perhaps the science test was highly conceptual while the mathematics test focused only on simple computation. It might even be that on the day of the science test Jason was coming down with the flu. The fact of the matter is that there are any number of reasons that might account for the difference between the science and arithmetic scores other than a difference in Jason's relative ability in the two subjects. An adequate evaluation of his ability must take these possibilities into account.

Decision making is an evaluative process; it involves making value judgments about the information upon which the decision is to be made. Sometimes, the judgments will be limited to what measures to use and, perhaps, the minimum criteria for selection. At other times, the judgments will extend to a consideration of the reliability and validity of particular measurement instruments for assessing the ability of a particular child. The nature of the evaluative process will depend upon the type of decision that needs to be made.

Educational decisions are involved in grading, diagnosing student needs, deciding placement and selection, planning instruction, and determining program offerings. While some of these decisions are based upon the diagnosis of an individual child's abilities, others depend upon group performance. In deciding whether or not Douglas should be placed in an accelerated science program, for example, we would be concerned with his performance in science. In deciding whether the experimental science program should be continued, we would not be concerned with a particular child's performance but with the overall performance of all the children in the program. In making the latter type of decision, we would not be concerned with the reliability and validity of our instruments for a particular child or the extenuating circumstances that might have affected that child's performance; the likelihood is that the measurement error in one child's score will be balanced by the error in another's. For this type of decision, then, we should be more concerned with the validity of the measurement instruments for assessing the objectives of the program.

Even when we are concerned with making decisions about individual students, however, there are times when it is inappropriate to permit extenuating circumstances to affect the decision. If, for example, a scholarship is awarded on the basis of an essay contest, the decision should be made solely on an evaluation of the essays. In this case, the essay must stand on its own merits. Although one might question whether an essay contest is the best basis on which to award a scholarship, the decision as to who will get the scholarship should not take into account extenuating circumstances that might have affected the quality of a particular child's submission.

Although we must be aware that any one score may not be representative of a child's ability, this awareness should not always affect the decisions that are made. The extent to which extenuating factors should enter into the decision depends upon the nature of the decision.

SELECTION AND PLACEMENT DECISIONS

Selection and placement decisions involve setting admission and retention criteria for different classes, programs, or schools as well as evaluating the extent to which a particular student meets those criteria. Sometimes these decisions are simple and are based on clear, objective data. If, for example, the state requires students who fall below the fourth stanine on a reading achievement test to receive remedial reading services, the selection decision involves simply identifying those youngsters who scored below the fourth stanine. At other times, however, these decisions may be quite complex.

Assume, for example, that the middle school that Jessica attends offers an accelerated program in mathematics that enables students to complete the standard ninth grade mathematics course by the end of eighth grade. The requirements for acceptance into the program include scholastic aptitude test performance at or above the 95th percentile on national norms, a stanine of 9 on a standardized mathematics achievement test given at the end of fifth grade, and a positive teacher recommendation.

Jessica has always been a top student in mathematics; her grades have always been excellent, her teachers have consistently cited her outstanding grasp of mathematical concepts, and she has invariably scored at the 98th or 99th percentiles on the mathematics subtests of the achievement test battery that is annually administered in her school district. Jessica has not been accepted for the accelerated mathematics program, however, because she does not meet all of the criteria. Although she was recommended by her teacher and her mathematics achievement scores fell in the ninth stanine, her scholastic aptitude test score was only at the 94th percentile.

This situation raises several issues regarding selection criteria. Based on the discussion of validity and reliability in Chapters 2 and 3, one would clearly recommend that decisions be based on more than the score on a single test. We would want to base important decisions on information from a variety of sources; we would want to use multiple criteria. The use of a combination of aptitude and achievement tests combined with teacher recommendations is quite common and is not necessarily a problem. The problem lies in how these multiple criteria are applied.

In the above example, a child must meet the minimum on each of the separate criteria in order to be accepted for the program. In such a process, each separate measure takes on equal importance and any one of the measures, regardless of its weaknesses or limitations, can bar a child's acceptance. Although such procedures are widely used in the elementary and secondary schools, they are seriously flawed.

The argument for multiple criteria is that we do not want to base important educational decisions on a single measure. No assessment is perfectly reliable and, in order to obtain valid measures of complex abilities, we may need a number of distinct measures, some of which will be less reliable than others. We know that the information obtained from any one measure may be inaccurate and hope that, by using information from a variety of sources, we will get a more reliable assessment of the ability in question. Ideally, multiple measures should be used in such a way that the information obtained from each measure enhances and supplements, rather than supplants, the other available information.

When the selection process requires a child to obtain a minimum score on each criterion, however, the score on the least reliable measure may be the deciding factor. In the above situation, it may not be the least reliable measure that bars Jessica from the program but it is the score on a single measure—the scholastic aptitude test—that is the deciding factor. Her other scores may have been the highest in the school, and she may have received the strongest teacher recommendation in her grade. These assessments don't count, however, when she falls below the criterion on the aptitude test. It is that one aptitude test score that bars her from the program.

Using multiple criteria in this manner defeats the purpose of multiple measures and often results, de facto, in basing a selection decision on a single measure. Other ways of dealing with multiple criteria are preferable. One alternative is to average the scores on the various measures. The advantage of a procedure such as this is that each score contributes to the average, and high scores on one measure may compensate for low scores on another. Even using a procedure such as this, however, there are problems. Not only is there often difficulty in determining just how much weight should be assigned to each of the measures, but an unreliable score on any one of the measures can unduly affect the result.

Furthermore, neither approach makes allowance for error in the scores. Each student's scores are treated as valid and reliable; there is no evaluation of the information provided. Jessica's aptitude test score may have been spuriously low in view of her other scores, but this factor was not taken into account. What if she wasn't feeling well when she was tested? Or what if there had been a timing or a scoring error on the test? When decisions about an individual student are made solely on the basis of a set of scores without consideration of the validity and reliability of those scores for the individual, the decision may be made on the basis of an inaccurate assessment of the student's abilities.

The rationale that is often given for using such procedures is that they are fair, that the decisions would be biased if factors other than the scores themselves were taken into account. It is true, of course, that if extenuating circumstances were to be considered, the decision would become more subjective. Biases may creep into subjective decisions, but such decisions are not inherently unfair. Guidelines and criteria may be established for handling situations in which the scores are suspect. One approach is to allow retesting if a student meets all the criteria but one. Another is to retest all students who fall less than one standard error of measurement below the criterion. In other cases, selection may not require a student to meet each of the separate criteria. Acceptance may be contingent on meeting three out of four criteria or exceeding a specified score on four out of five criteria. In still other instances, a selection committee may be given the discretion to make decisions about students who don't meet all the criteria.

It should also be noted, of course, that selection and placement decisions are not always based on a combination of objective scores. There are many instances when decisions are made on the basis of such subjective information as teacher recommendations, the recommendations of a school psychologist or guidance counselor, or the evaluation of a selection committee. Even college admissions decisions are often made on the basis of a subjective evaluation of each applicant's credentials. Although a student's high school average and scores on standardized achievement and/or aptitude tests are considered, other factors may account for one student being accepted when other students with higher scores are not. Test scores and the high school average are evaluated in relationship to the high school program that the student took as well as other activities in which the student may have been involved. Other information about the student is used to supplement the scores; it provides a more valid assessment of the student's strengths and weaknesses.

Not only can subjective data add to the information provided by objective measures and enhance the validity of the assessment, but there are some abilities for which there are no valid objective measures. How would you select youngsters for a program in musical performance? Or in art? When subjective measures are used, however, the criteria on which the decision is to be made should be clearly articulated, and every attempt should be made to assess those criteria in as valid and reliable manner as possible. Procedures should be adopted, for example, that minimize bias. Wherever possible, more than one person should assess the credentials, the same criteria should be impartially applied to each person's credentials, and the decision should not be influenced by extraneous personal knowledge of the applicants.

As mentioned above, however, there are times when objective decision rules are necessary, and it would be counterproductive to evaluate the reliability and validity of each individual's scores. When, for example, scholarships are awarded on the basis of a competitive examination, we don't expect any special consideration if Michael had a stomachache on the day of the test or Jeremy was overly anxious and didn't do as well as he could have. Similarly, when a minimum competency test is required for a diploma, we don't expect the criterion to be changed for a child who didn't perform as well as expected. In some such cases, the opportunity is lost. In others, the test is taken again at another time. We must realize, however, that these decisions are not made on the basis of the best possible assessment of each child's abilities. The child who wins the scholarship is not necessarily a better student than the one who doesn't, and the child who passes the minimum competency examination may not be any more competent than one who scores just below the criterion. Using a single score as the basis for these decisions reflects administrative—or often political—concerns rather than the best assessment practice.

GRADING DECISIONS

Grades are most useful when they indicate the extent to which a child has attained the objectives of instruction. As with any educational decision, grading decisions should be based on as much information as possible. The information on which a grade is based, however, should be germane to the child's mastery of the material taught in class.

In those cases in which a single letter or numerical grade is given, the grade loses its usefulness as a measure of achievement if extra credit toward a grade is given for behavior that doesn't signify attainment of the learning objectives. If, for example, Richard is having difficulty in algebra, his algebra grade should reflect the degree to which he has mastered algebra; it should not be raised because he is trying hard, attending extra-help sessions, being cooperative in class, or participating in volunteer activities. These other behaviors may be commendable, but they do not indicate his mastery of algebra. Similarly, if grades are lowered for disruptive behavior, sloppy work, or inappropriate dress, the grade loses its usefulness as a measure of achievement.

That is not to say that these other behaviors are not important or that they should not be reported to parents. The question is how to do so without compromising the meaning of the grade. In many schools, there are separate grades given for these behaviors. A student may receive a grade in achievement as well as in conduct, effort, or attitude toward school.

When a single grade is given, it provides a global measure of the child's achievement; it doesn't indicate the child's strengths and weaknesses or specific areas in which extra help may be needed. For this reason, many schools use grade reports that not only enable the teacher to give different grades for achievement and classroom behavior, but also allow for separate grades in different areas of achievement. In reading, for example, separate grades may be given for comprehension, word attack skills, reading speed, and oral reading skill. In some schools, a checklist of skills is provided for each subject and the teacher rates the child on each objective.

Other schools provide for more in-depth reporting through narrative reports and parent-teacher conferences. Although these methods of reporting student progress enable a more detailed assessment than can a single grade, the areas of assessment tend to be inconsistent from child to child and from time to time. The narrative may focus on Jason's reading progress one time and his study skills the next. And Michael's conference may focus only on his disruptive behavior in class. Unless there is some consistency in what is being addressed, it is very difficult to track a child's development over time. This type of reporting is most valuable when the report or conference focuses on a specified set of criteria.

Regardless of the form of the grade report, most grading decisions are primarily based on criterion-referenced assessments. All those students who meet the criterion score for a particular grade are assigned that grade. If scores of 90 to 100 are assigned a grade of A, every student scoring above a 90 will receive an A. Rarely does a teacher arbitrarily decide, for example, that the top 20% of the class will receive grades of A regardless of the extent to which they master the course objectives. Although some schools will provide guidelines indicating the proportion of students in a typical class expected to receive each letter grade, the distribution of grades is usually dependent on the ability and achievement of the class. In a high-achieving class, where most students do well on the tests, there will usually be more A and B grades than in a class in which the students do not perform as well.

It should be noted, however, that even though most grades are primarily criterion-referenced, the criteria are rarely well specified. Grading systems are often arbitrary; although grades from 90 to 100% on a test may be assigned a letter grade of A, there is rarely a clear specification of exactly what skills a child with a 95 on a test or a grade of A has mastered. Although such grades provide a general impression of a child's level of performance, they do not clearly specify the child's strengths and weaknesses. Nor are they directly comparable across subjects or teachers. One teacher's A may be another's B, and a 95 in a tenth grade English course may not represent any greater mastery of the course material than does a 90 in an eleventh grade English course.

Although one hears students speak of "grading on a curve," it is very rare for classroom grades to be assigned this way. Technically, to grade on a curve is to assign grades in such a way that the percentage of students receiving each grade is equivalent to the percentage of students that would receive that grade if the grades formed a normal distribution, as described in Chapter 9. In fact, when teachers say that they are curving the scores or grading on a curve, they usually mean that they are adjusting the scores to account for an unexpectedly difficult test. If, for example, a teacher knows that about a quarter of the students usually get scores above 90 and finds that, on a particular test, none of the students scored this high, the teacher may add 5 or 10 points to each student's score. Alternatively, the teacher may say that, although scores from 80 to 90 are usually considered equivalent to a grade of A, scores from 80 to 90 will be equivalent to an A on this particular test.

Although grades are usually criterion-referenced, this type of adjustment reflects a norm-referenced judgment. There is an intuitive comparison between the actual performance of the class and the performance expected of similar classes. Such adjustments may be appropriate when a test is unusually difficult and students have, in fact, mastered the material to the same level of proficiency as in other similar classes. In other instances, this practice may mask the fact that the students did not master the material.

There is no one answer as to how to handle this problem or how to determine whether the problem stems from the test or from the students' level of proficiency. Whether or not a test score is representative of a student's achievement is a subjective judgment. The best indicator of the representativeness of any particular test score, whether for an individual student or for a class, is the degree to which it is consistent with other information. If the students appear to understand the material in class, are successfully completing their assignments, and are making appropriate progress in class, unusually low scores on a test are more likely to reflect a problem with the test than with the students.

Similarly, even if the class as a whole performs as expected, if a student who appears to be doing well in class and understands the work does unusually poorly on a test, the score may not be an accurate reflection of that student's achievement. If the problem were limited to one student, however, a teacher would not add points to the student's score. One way teachers may handle such eventualities is to drop each child's lowest score when computing the average. In other cases, children may be allowed to repeat a test.

Whatever procedure is followed, the aim is for each child's grade to accurately reflect that child's mastery of the material taught. We don't want one inaccurate score to result in a grade that gives a distorted picture of the student's achievement. We also want the grade to reflect the level of mastery on all of the important learning objectives. In a science course, for example, where students are learning laboratory skills, an assessment of their laboratory work should be included in the grade. Similarly, in a social studies course in which students are learning research skills, their mastery of these skills should also contribute to their grade.

Furthermore, in arriving at a grade, it is important to give appropriate weight to the different learning objectives. The most important objectives should contribute most to the score. If in a French course, for example, the emphasis is on developing facility in speaking the language, the grade should not be based primarily on paper-and-pencil grammar tests. Although a child's skill in speaking the language may be difficult to assess, the grade will not provide a valid evaluation of the student's mastery of the course objectives unless this skill is appropriately reflected in the grade.

To be most useful, then, a grade should be a valid and reliable representation of the extent to which a child has mastered the objectives of instruction. The grading process is an evaluation process; judgments must be made not only about the knowledge and skills to be measured, but also about the measurement procedures to be used and the way in which the sources of information are to be combined.

DIAGNOSTIC, INSTRUCTIONAL, AND PROGRAM DECISIONS

Not all educational decisions involve placement, selection, or the assignment of grades. There are times when day-to-day instructional decisions are based on a diagnosis of a particular child's strengths and weaknesses and times when the overall performance of a class will affect curriculum and program development. For example, when a child appears to have a persistent learning problem, an individual diagnostic evaluation may be indicated. A teacher may also want to diagnose each child's strengths and weaknesses in order to most effectively form instructional groups. At other times, the test performance of a group of students may lead to decisions involving curriculum modification or program offerings.

In either type of situation, the test as well as the score must be evaluated. Not only should we evaluate the overall validity and reliability of the test scores but, when assessing individual students, we should always look for patterns of consistency. If Andrew receives a low score on the standardized reading test administered in first grade, for example, we cannot immediately conclude that he is having difficulty learning to read. We must question whether that score is representative of his work in class and whether there are any other indications of a reading problem. An isolated low score should not be ignored; unexpected test performance should not be dismissed without further investigation, but the score alone should not be taken as the final arbiter of a student's achievement or ability. Although test scores may help in identifying a problem area or diagnosing a child's strengths and weaknesses, a thorough diagnosis of a suspected problem requires more than a single test.

In the case of a consistent learning problem, a child should receive a comprehensive diagnostic evaluation. This evaluation should include the assessment of the classroom teacher, parents, and others who know the child as well as the professional judgment of the school psychologist. It should include in-depth diagnostic testing and, perhaps, a referral for an assessment of neurological functioning. Each individual test score may provide valuable information, but that information must be evaluated as part of the decision-making process. As previously emphasized, it is not only the meaning of each score that must be understood but the nature of the information provided. Patterns must be discerned and the reliability and validity of the information must be assessed in light of what is known about the child.

Diagnostic decisions are not limited, of course, to situations where learning problems are suspected. Teachers regularly make day-to-day instructional decisions on the basis of students' test performance. Although the diagnosis of a learning problem calls for a more formal and comprehensive evaluation than do day-to-day instructional decisions, the guiding principles should be the same. Although a standardized arithmetic or reading score may be used for determining the initial level of instruction in a class, classroom performance, as well as other available information about the child, should also be considered. A test score should not replace a teacher's professional judgment; instead, the teacher's assessment of the child's classroom performance should supplement the test score. The test score represents the child's performance on a single day; the teacher's knowledge of the student and how the child performs in class over time provides a wealth of additional information. Where test scores and classroom assessment agree, they confirm each other. Where there are disparities, further investigation of the causes is warranted. There are times when the test score will reveal strengths and problems of which the teacher wasn't aware, and there will be times when the test score will inaccurately portray a child's ability. The evaluation process should enable the teacher to distinguish between the two.

In addition to instructional decisions about an individual child, the teacher or the school may also make curriculum decisions based on group performance. If the third grade as a whole, for example, is falling below the norm in reading, the school may wish to revise the reading curriculum. If tenth-graders are doing exceptionally well on standardized mathematics tests, an accelerated mathematics program may be initiated. Within a particular class, poor performance on a classroom test may result in more time for review or extra work on some skills.

When scores of a large group of children, rather than those of an individual child, are considered, there are fewer concerns about the reliability of the test. Measurement error associated with the scores of individual children tend to cancel each other out. The question of validity, however, remains in the forefront. If, for example, the third graders are doing poorly on standardized reading tests, one has to question why. Is it that there are problems with the curriculum? Or is the test outdated? Does the curriculum focus on skills not covered on the test? With respect to poor performance on a classroom test, the teacher has to question whether the problem was the students' mastery of the work or whether it was with the test. Was the material particularly complex and difficult to learn? Or was the test so poorly constructed that the students couldn't demonstrate what they knew? As in all evaluation, the test scores provide only one source of information, and this information cannot be viewed in isolation.

In effect, all tests are used for evaluation purposes. They provide measures of individual and group performance that are used in arriving at educational decisions. A particular test score, however, is simply one source of information. In evaluating that information, consideration should be given to the type of information provided by the score, the characteristics of the test, and the testing situation.

Tests do provide useful information, but they also have their limitations, limitations that must be considered when test scores are used in educational decision making. A test score doesn't necessarily tell the truth about an individual; we should neither blindly put our faith in test scores nor discard them for not meeting all our expectations. Instead, we should use them judiciously and put them in their proper place in the evaluation process.

Appendix

Where to Find Information about Published Tests

REFERENCE BOOKS

Murphy, Linda L., Conoley, Jane Close, and Impara, James C. (forthcoming). *Tests in Print IV*. Lincoln, Neb.: The Buros Institute of Mental Measurements of the University of Nebraska.

Tests in Print IV is the latest version of *Tests in Print*, which lists all published testing instruments available at the time of printing. The listing includes the publisher and date of publication of each testing instrument as well as references to reviews of the instrument in the *Mental Measurements Yearbook (MMY)*. A list of test publishers is also included.

Kramer, Jack J., and Conoley, Jane Close (Eds.) (1992). *The Eleventh Mental Measurements Yearbook*. Lincoln, Neb.: The Buros Institute of Mental Measurements of the University of Nebraska.

The Eleventh Mental Measurements Yearbook includes reviews of recently published tests, usually by two independent reviewers. Also included is descriptive information about the test, bibliographies of articles about the test and excerpts from reviews of the test in journals. The *Yearbooks* are updated every few years and supplements are published in between; *The Twelfth Mental Measurements Yearbook* is forthcoming. Since each *Yearbook* focuses on tests published since the last volume, it is often necessary to look at several volumes for reviews of all the major tests in a particular area. There is also a *Mental Measurements Yearbook* database that offers updated information on tests; the database may be accessed through Bibliographic Retrieval Services, Inc. (BRS), an on-line computer service offered through many libraries.

Sweetland, Richard C., and Keyser, Daniel J. (Eds.) (1991). *Tests: A Comprehensive Reference for Assessments in Psychology, Education and Business* (3d ed.). Austin, Tex.: Pro-Ed.

While *Tests* does not include evaluative reviews, it does provide a comprehensive listing of published tests in psychology, education, and business. Each listing includes a description of the test, its purpose, and the publisher.

Keyser, Daniel J., and Sweetland, Richard C. (Eds.) (1992). *Test Critiques: Volume X*. Austin, Tex.: Pro-Ed.

Each volume of *Test Critiques* includes detailed reviews of a number of tests. The reviews include technical information, such as validity and reliability data, as well as information about applications and administration of the test and an overall critique. Unlike the *Mental Measurements Yearbooks*, however, there is only one review of each test.

PROFESSIONAL JOURNALS

In addition to the reference books cited above, several professional journals also include reviews of tests. References to test reviews in the professional journals may be found in *Psychological Abstracts*, *Education Index*, *Current Index to Journals in Education (CIJE)*, and *Resources in Education (RIE)*.

EDUCATIONAL TESTING SERVICE (ETS) *TEST COLLECTION BIBLIOGRAPHIES*

ETS has a very extensive collection of both published and unpublished tests. The *Test Collection Bibliographies* provide a description of each of the tests as well as the publisher and date of publication. There are separate *Bibliographies* for different types of tests.

TEST PUBLISHERS' CATALOGUES

Test publishers distribute catalogues that provide descriptive information on the tests they publish. The catalogues usually include a description of the test, its purpose and target population, and ordering information. A complete list of test publishers may be found in *Tests in Print*.

Bibliography

Airasian, P. W. (1991). *Classroom assessment.* New York: McGraw-Hill.

Cunningham, G. K. (1986). *Educational and psychological measurement.* New York: Macmillan.

Gronlund, N. L., and Linn, R. L. (1990). *Measurement and evaluation in teaching* (6th ed.). New York: Macmillan.

Keyser, D. J., and Sweetland, R. C. (Eds.) (1984). *Test critiques.* Kansas City, Mo.: Test Corporation of America.

Kubiszyn, T., and Borich, G. (1993). *Educational testing and measurement* (4th ed.). New York: HarperCollins.

Mehrens, W. A., and Lehman, I. J. (1987). *Using standardized tests in education* (4th ed.). New York: Longman.

Oosterhof, A. (1994). *Classroom applications of educational measurement* (2d ed.). New York: Macmillan.

Sweetland, R. C., and Keyser, D. J. (Eds.) (1987). *Tests: a comprehensive reference for assessments in psychology, education and business* (2d ed.). Kansas City, Mo.: Test Corporation of America.

Thorndike, R. M.; Cunningham, G. K.; Thorndike, R. L.; and Hagen, E. P. (1991). *Measurement and evaluation in psychology and education* (5th ed.). New York: Macmillan.

Wiersma, W., and Jurs, S. G. (1990). *Educational measurement and testing* (2d ed.). Boston: Allyn and Bacon.

Worthen, B.; Borg, W. R.; and White, K. R. (1993). *Measurement and evaluation in the schools*. New York: Longman.

Index

About the Author

ESTELLE S. GELLMAN is Professor of Counseling, Research, Special Education, and Rehabilitation at Hofstra University in Hempstead, New York. She is the author of two textbooks for teachers on the use of statistics.